Business Communications

HARPERCOLLINS COLLEGE OUTLINE

Business Communications

Claudia Rawlins, Ph.D.
California State University at Chico

HarperPerennial
A Division of HarperCollins*Publishers*

FIRST HARPERPERENNIAL EDITION

Project Manager: Mary Mooney
Editor: Thomas H. Quinn

Library of Congress Cataloging-in-Publication Data
Rawlins, Claudia.
    Business communications / Claudia Rawlins.
        p.   cm.
    Includes bibliographical references.
    ISBN: 0-06-467155-0
    1. Business communication.   I. Title.
HF5718.R38   1993
658.4'5--dc20   92-54688

93 94 95 96 97 ◆/RRD 10 9 8 7 6 5 4 3 2 1

To my family:

Hans J. Däumer

Molly E. Rawlins

Kenneth W. Bensel

Dollie L. Bensel

You're the Greatest!

Contents

Preface

Dear Reader:

How well you communicate determines how well you live.

This book presents, in abbreviated form, what I believe to be the most crucial ingredients to effective communication. Their application will make your work easier and your homelife more caring.

Business Communications is part of the HarperCollins College Outline series. As with all the books in this series, it provides a summary of the topics essential to the first course in a field. You can use this book, along with an assigned textbook, to help clarify business communication topics. Headings, boldface and italic type make the book handy for review and exam preparation.

Business Communications is also complete enough to stand on its own, either as a course text or as a tool for self-study. Examples throughout the book and exercises at the end of chapters will help you put the principles discussed to work in your life. The bibliography suggests other books you might find helpful in developing your communication skills.

Many people helped in the process of getting this book into your hands. Their names don't appear on the title page, but their contributions were essential. Fred N. Grayson of American BookWorks is a saint. He knew when I needed a kind word and when I needed a kick in the pants. If you ever need a production editor, go to him.

Thomas H. Quinn of Quinn & Tuttle served as my editor. His kind words kept me at the keyboard. R. Burdette was the copy editor from whom I learned the difference between *as* and *like* and to whom I owe thanks for helping me improve my own writing. I appreciate the help of these professionals more than they know.

My family and friends were also instrumental in making this book a reality. I become obsessed when I'm writing a manuscript; their support remained constant. I'm lucky to have such wonderful people in my life.

I wish you great success in your study of business communications. My hope is that your work will become easier and more enjoyable as you gain skill at applying the ideas in this book.

Claudia Rawlins, Ph.D.

Business Communications

1

Communicating in the Global Organization

*B*usiness organizations are held together by networks of communication. Perhaps more than any other aspect of an organization, its communication determines how effective the organization is. The surest way to achieve effective organization-wide communication is to improve the communication skills of each individual in the organization. Individuals may have thorough knowledge of a technology or specialization, but if they fail to communicate their ideas and thoughts to others, they will find it difficult to achieve either organizational or personal goals.

New communication technologies, changing cultural expectations, an increasingly interdependent global marketplace, and growing concerns about the environment are all influencing what is meant by effective individual communication. Worldwide competition requires world-class communication. As a result, more will be asked of you as an individual communicator. Whatever your current communication skills, changing conditions in the workplace will encourage you to polish and perfect those skills.

This chapter provides a broad introduction to the issues that are part of modern business communication.

COMMUNICATION EFFECTIVENESS

Many researchers have investigated what distinguishes successful managers from unsuccessful managers. The overall conclusion of their studies is that effective communication is indispensable. Such studies have found that managers spend from 80 to 99 percent of their time communicating with others. Of this time, about 25 percent is spent resolving conflicts.

First-line managers spend more time supervising others than they spend on any other managerial function. Supervision largely entails communicating clearly with subordinates about their work. As managers move up the hierarchy to middle management, they must become experts of negotiation and conflict resolution. Improving interpersonal skills is often seen as a top priority for management training and development. At the top of the managerial hierarchy, communication skills remain critical since executives typically function by developing highly personal relationships with one another and relying on high levels of group involvement. At every level of management, persuasive skills are essential to "working with and through others"—the basic definition of management.

Effective communication includes written communication as well as face-to-face and electronic conversation. In a national survey of executives, 79 percent listed the ability to write as the most neglected skill in business. In this same group, 89 percent expressed the belief that clear writing demonstrates clear thinking.

Other studies have documented the benefits of effective communication skills not only for an individual manager's career but also for the organization in which he or she works. Communication effectiveness has been linked to increased efficiency, reduced grievances and absenteeism, increased satisfaction, and improved role clarity for subordinates. A 1988 survey of *Fortune 500* chief executive officers found that 97 percent of those surveyed believed their skill at communicating had a major influence on employee job satisfaction, 84 percent believed it improved employee job performance, and 71 percent believed it had a positive impact on profits.

Since effective interpersonal communication results in substantial benefits to the individual manager and the individual's organization, improving your interpersonal skills is clearly an important undertaking. By learning the material in this book, you will be taking large strides toward developing your own managerial effectiveness.

COMMUNICATION DEFINED

Communication is the transfer of meaning from a sender to a receiver. *Effective* communication implies that the meaning received is the meaning the sender *intended*.

For example, if your officemate takes a phone message for you and you are unable to tell if one of the numbers in the caller's phone number is a 1 or a 7, effective communication did not take place. If you smile at your boss intending to show approval of an idea, and your boss concludes you approve, effective communication has taken place.

An important quality of face-to-face communication is that it is *dynamic*. Messages are sent and received simultaneously. In addition to indicating to the sender that you understand, agree with, or are confused by a message, your nonverbal feedback can even persuade the sender to change the message in the middle. A subordinate might begin telling the boss about a new idea with enthusiasm. As the boss's face registers disagreement and irritation, the subordinate might end the message by saying "Of course, this idea is too expensive and won't work in this economic climate."

Communication Channels

A communication channel is the method or medium used by the sender to send the message. Examples of different channels include telephone call, voice mail, fax, face-to-face conversation, nonverbal hand signals, typed letter, and handwritten memo. As Marshall McLuhan first suggested in the 1960s, messages are affected by the medium. A message in writing is likely to seem more formal and rigid than the same message delivered in a face-to-face conversation.

COMMUNICATING IN WRITING

Different channels provide different specific benefits. Written communication allows the receiver to go over the message as frequently as needed to digest the meaning. As a result, written communication is especially suited to delivering complex information. Researchers have noted that older people prefer to receive their information in writing because it is self-paced: the reader can determine the speed with which the information is received.

Writing also provides a lasting record of a communication, and so is preferred in situations where a record is important, such as ordering materials, bidding on contracts, communicating policies and procedures, and hiring employees.

On the negative side, writing takes longer. Most people find that developing clear written messages is especially challenging. First, a written message is effective only if it gets read, so the writer must be concerned about readability. Second, although the writer can take the time to write and rewrite the message, the writer ultimately has only one chance to make the message clear to the reader—the writer must develop the message and deliver it without receiving any feedback.

TELEPHONE COMMUNICATION

The telephone provides quick access. As a result, it is frequently faster and less expensive than written communication or face-to-face interaction. Researchers have concluded that telephone communicators have a difficult time camouflaging untruths. In other words, if you want to know if a particular person is telling you the truth, talk to that person over the phone. Careful listening will give you strong voice-quality clues to the veracity of what the other is saying. Changes in speaking rate, tonal quality, and loudness rapidly communicate emotion. If you the know the normal voice quality of a person, you can sense when the person is tense. Such tension supports your hypothesis that the person is lying.

VIDEO CONFERENCING

Video conferencing is a communication channel available at many worksites. Both voice and picture are sent over a distance. Newscasts make frequent use of video conferencing to interview newsmakers in distant cities or countries. Companies use video conferencing, for example, to make simultaneous announcements to subsidiaries worldwide or interview job candidates in other cities. U.S. telephone companies have recently made picture phones available for household use. Currently, these telephones cost about $1,500.

Researchers have made some interesting observations about the impact of the video-conferencing channel on communication. In spite of the addition of the picture, video-conferencing participants experience the communication much as they experience voice-only telephone calls. Video conferencing is much more like the telephone than like face-to-face conversation.

FACE-TO-FACE COMMUNICATION

Communication with someone who is right in front of you has many advantages. First, feedback is instantaneous. When your message is misunderstood, you have the immediate opportunity to clarify it. Second, you can use nonverbal messages to add impact to your verbal message. Largely as a result of nonverbal messages, face-to-face communication leaves communicators with an emotional impression as well as the rational meaning of the message. Third, research indicates that face-to-face communication allows a sender who so chooses to control and influence a situation. Nonverbal signals allow the sender to reduce interruptions and retain control of the conversation. Additionally, face-to-face communication is the most interactive communication channel. Sending and receiving can go on simultaneously. The messages of one communicator build rapidly on the messages of the other communicators.

Silence is an effective way to communicate certain points. When communicators are face-to-face, silence communicates clearly. When they are not face-to-face, the silence can more easily be misinterpreted. Not receiving a letter from someone may mean she is angry at you. On the other hand, it may mean she forgot to mail the letter.

As an effective communicator, you can consciously consider the goals of your communication and choose the channel that will best help you achieve those goals.

Verbal and Nonverbal Communication

Communication has both verbal and nonverbal elements.

VERBAL COMMUNICATION

Verbal communication refers to the *words* a communicator chooses and the order in which the words are presented. Of all the different personal traits a person may possess, the only one which is consistently correlated with managerial or leadership skill is "size of vocabulary." The larger a person's vocabulary, the more likely it is that he or she will be an excellent manager. Researchers hypothesize that a large vocabulary allows a manager to choose just the right words for a particular situation.

In spite of this finding, researchers have concluded that the verbal portion of any communication transmits only 7 to 25 percent of the meaning. A much greater portion is transmitted nonverbally.

NONVERBAL COMMUNICATION

The **nonverbal** elements of communication include the following.

Voiced nonverbals. Sounds like *Ugh!*, *Um. . .*, *Whew,* and *Yipes!* add a great deal of meaning to a message. They are not literally words, even though we have agreed on more or less standard ways to spell and write them in dialogue. Voiced nonverbals are nonword sounds.

Voice quality. Speaking rate, voice volume, voice quality, and accent are all powerful elements of communication. As O. J. Simpson and Barbara Walters are aware, learning to control the elements of voice quality can have a tremendous impact on your communication effectiveness. These two people, who had very distinctive accents compared to the standard television commentator, worked with voice coaches to change their voice quality, and both have prospered in television as a result.

A louder than usual voice usually indicates excitement; a very rapid speaking rate is an indicator of nervousness. Different accents often add information about the geographic or socioeconomic background of the speaker.

Body language. Where the communicators can see each other, a significant portion of the message is transmitted through body movements. The eyes, face, hands, and overall posture are especially powerful elements of communication. Body size, muscle tone, and perceived attractiveness also influence how a communicator's message is received and interpreted.

Personal symbols. What a person wears, its style, quality, and cleanliness, communicates a great deal about the person's profession and status. Jewelry, hairstyle, and perfume contribute to the message. Advertisers use this observation to sell an "image" with their products.

Nonverbals in written communication. Even when the communication is in writing, nonverbal cues influence meaning. The quality of the paper, whether the message is handwritten or typed, the darkness of the type, the particular style and size of the type, even the size and ink color of the signature, become part of the total message.

BARRIERS TO EFFECTIVE COMMUNICATION

The desire to communicate is inborn. The youngest baby cries in an attempt to communicate that something is wrong. However the desire to communicate does not lead infallibly to the ability to communicate effectively. Many personal, structural, and organizational barriers get in the way. Understanding the barriers is an important first step in overcoming them.

Language

Language, and how we use it, can lead to effective communication or can erect barriers to understanding. Counting professional and technical terms, the English language has about 800,000 words. Most adults conduct their daily conversations using no more than 10,000 words, and it is possible to make yourself understood in most situations using a 1,000-word vocabulary. However, a person who speaks using 1,000 or 2,000 words will have trouble understanding the speech of someone who chooses a different 2,000-word set. The communicator with a larger vocabulary has the ability to reach a much broader audience.

DENOTATION AND CONNOTATION

In addition to the large number of possible words, words frequently have both a denotative and a connotative meaning. The **denotative** meaning is the literal, or dictionary, meaning. For example, the word *desk* brings to mind a certain type of furniture. Sometimes, the denotative meaning is known as the *labeling* meaning.

The **connotative** meaning of a word includes all the associations and feelings the word evokes. It is the *emotional* meaning. For example, the content of the sets of sentences that follow is the same. The feelings the two versions evoke in you, however, are very different.

Example 1.1

You failed the exam.
You achieved 65 percent on the exam.

In your letter, you state that the toaster will not brown four slices of
  bread at once.
In your letter, you claim that the toaster will not brown four slices of
  bread at once.
B.B. returned to the house.
B.B. returned home.

Emotion-laden language can rapidly lead to miscommunication
because sender and receiver are less likely to experience the same emotional response. For example, when one person hears "claim" as "I don't
believe you," and the other hears it as "stated," the two will have very different expectations for the outcome of the communication. "Home" in the
last pair communicates a "place where he feels comfortable." "The house"
could be any place where people live. The effective communicator tries to
use words that have very little connotative meaning.

ABSTRACTION AND CONCRETENESS

In addition to varying in connotative impact, words also vary in their
level of abstraction. An abstract word expresses a concept, quality, or characteristic. **Abstractions** are usually broad, encompassing an entire category
of ideas. Examples of abstract words include *honor, trust, democracy,
patriotism, motivation, productivity*, and *heritage*.

When a word is **concrete**, it is anchored in the tangible world we can
experience with our senses. Concrete words stand for something in particular. Examples of concrete words include *chair, tooth, building, cat, car,* and
computer.

The level of abstraction can be adjusted. For example, *acquaintance* is
quite abstract, *colleague* less abstract, *office partner* even more concrete,
and *Rebecca* very concrete. Business communicators will reduce barriers
by providing enough concrete language to clarify what they mean by the
more abstract words they use.

POLARIZATION AND STATIC TENDENCIES

English has literally thousands of pairs of adjectives that describe
opposites. Some examples include *hot-cold, tall-short, first-last, good-bad,*
and *wise-foolish*. These pairs are called polar opposites, and they lead to a
barrier of communication known as polarization. **Polarization** is the tendency to perceive things in the extreme. When we say "Paul is foolish," we
are not being accurate. Paul, like all humans, is sometimes wise and sometimes foolish, and most of the time his behavior falls somewhere between
those polar opposites. However, the shape of the language encourages
polarization. Effective communicators can counteract this tendency by saying "Paul can be foolish" or being more concrete and descriptive: "Paul

acted foolishly on Saturday evening when he arrived an hour late to the dinner."

English also has the tendency to encourage speakers to make static statements. A *static tendency* results from the word *is,* which freezes statements in a never-changing condition. *Is* implies "always was, always will be," even when we do not want to mean that. For example, "Michele is messy" seems to freeze Michele into a role from which she cannot escape. S. I. Hayakawa, a noted linguist, suggested that to overcome the barrier of our static language, we add the date. "On June 12, Michele is messy." Although this advice may not always seem appropriate, it does remind us that what *is* will most likely not *always be.*

Psychological Barriers

Both the sender and receiver are affected by their psychological states. When either communicator is angry, depressed, afraid, or defensive, the communication is certain to contain significant decoding and encoding noise. As an example, imagine an employee, Roberto, whose best friend was suddenly fired from his job this week. Roberto has been worried about his friend and worried that this trauma might happen to him. When Roberto's boss stops by and says, "Roberto, I'd like you to drop by my office this afternoon," Roberto is more likely to interpret the request with fear than with pride. Although not always possible, communicating when you are in a good mood will reduce psychological barriers to effective communication.

Physical Barriers

The physical environment within which the communicators function can cause significant barriers to effective communication. Lawnmowers outside the window, assembly equipment on the shop floor, telephones ringing in the background, and other conversations in the vicinity are all environmental factors that often serve as barriers to effective communication. Whenever possible, the effective communicator chooses a quiet environment where the communicators are undisturbed by outside noise.

Some physical barriers are more structural than noisy. When management and union meet to discuss the new contract, they will be more confrontational if they sit across the table from each other than if they sit around a round table. When committee members meet around a large rectangular table, the person at the head of the table is likely to be seen as having the most power.

Physiological Barriers

Physiological barriers can also arise in individual communicators. For example, approximately 20 million Americans suffer significant hearing loss. Most of them rely on lipreading. That's nearly 10 percent of the population. Background sounds and inability to see the other's face significantly hamper communication effectiveness. Other internal physiological barriers might include hunger or pain, which distract the communicator from concentrating on the message. Gender-specific differences, differences that are the result of male patterns of communication versus female patterns, and degree of physical attractiveness are additional physiological factors that may contribute to physiological barriers to effective communication.

CONTEMPORARY ISSUES IN BUSINESS COMMUNICATION

Communication skills have always been important to managers, but their importance is growing. The *industrial age* manager (1880–1960) acted as a decision maker, whereas today's manager functions as an information processor. Many observers of today's technology and ways of doing business refer to our present economy as the *information age*. Information has become *central* to organizational operations; handling and transforming information is what most companies in the United States do. Information processing is essentially communication. Because information is now doubling every year and information can be transmitted worldwide by satellite instantly, our communication abilities are being tested. New managerial demands require new communication strategies.

International and Intercultural Communication

The United States is now the leading importer and the second-leading exporter of goods and services in the world. The fact that most business organizations will operate in an international environment increases the complexity of business communication. English is spoken by only 8.5 percent of the world's population.

Even those organizations that limit their operations to the United States face additional communication challenges that are the result of increased cultural diversity. Thirty percent of those who live in New York City were born outside the United States. Sixty-seven percent of Miami is Hispanic. Thirty-three percent of San Francisco is Asian. In California, English is the second language of nearly half the population. Such language and cultural diversity results in widespread translation (or coding and decoding) problems. However, there is much you can do to reduce miscommunication. The following communication *strategies* can help contemporary business communicators.

Maintain formality. In much of the world, the use of titles and formal names is more important than in the United States. As a result, the best contemporary communicators will err on the side of formality. Use a person's first name only if you have been asked to do so. Make sure you use professional and educational titles. For example, in Germany it would not be unusual to list all educational degrees when addressing a person. "Herr Professor Doktor Peter Karl Weber, Diplome Engineer" would be the proper way to address a male university professor who has a master's in engineering and a doctorate.

Avoid slang and idiomatic language. *Slang* is informal speech, understood because the people who use it share a great deal of background and experience. For example, *major* clearly communicates *good* to American teens. However, it is not found in the dictionary, so without personal experience with the word, no translation is possible. An *idiom* is an expression which means something other than the direct translation of the words. *To blow one's top* means "to be angry." For people new to a language, idioms and slang make accurate decoding especially difficult.

Show respect. Cross-cultural communication will be more accurate if the communicators begin with an attitude of respect. An active interest in learning about the other—his or her culture, language, and experiences—will indicate respect.

Be flexible. Each culture is somewhat ethnocentric. Its citizens believe that the way they do things is the best way. To communicate effectively across cultures, it may be necessary to try someone else's way. For example, the Japanese allow people to save face by not pressuring them to say no. U.S. communicators working in Japan will be more successful if they learn the subtle, indirect ways the Japanese reject an idea rather than pushing for yes-or-no decisions. Flexibility will take the cross-cultural communicator far in reducing misunderstanding.

Communicate clearly. Language can be used loosely, without precision. In the best of situations, failure to take responsibility for communicating clearly is likely to result in misunderstanding. When multiple language and cultural backgrounds add to the complexity of the communication, unclear communication has little chance of being interpreted as the sender intended. The following recommendations can add clarity to any communication:

1. Use concrete language. Rather than "Let's get together this afternoon," say "Please come over to my office at 3:00." Instead of "many customers prefer our new product," say "73% of our customers prefer the blue binding." Being more specific and concrete reduces the possibility of misinterpretation.

2. Use examples. The addition of a specific "for instance" allows the receiver to test whether he or she understood the general idea. When an organization develops a policy, employees will understand what is expected of them better if the general policy is followed by one or more examples. Suppose a policy manual says that "employees are expected to dress professionally." Employees might interpret "profes-

sionally" differently. Providing specific examples of what the company means by professional dress will help an employee decide what to wear. The policy might be followed by "Women's skirts must fall at or below the knee. Men are expected to wear a tie at all times. All employees are asked not to wear shorts, no matter how hot the weather."

3. Speak slowly and plainly. In all languages, many words sound similar. For example, the difference between *desert* and *dessert* and *pen* and *pin* is minor, yet the meaning is very different. Speaking clearly and slowly will assist the receiver to hear carefully. (Talking louder is not particularly helpful. In fact, most people tense up when they feel "yelled at," and their understanding declines rather than improves.)

4. Avoid humor. So much of what we think is funny is culturally determined. And humor that is misunderstood is often taken as criticism or being laughed at. Until you are certain your receiver will "hear" your humor the way you intended it, avoid making jokes or puns. Satire is especially likely to be misinterpreted as an insult.

5. Seek and provide feedback. Check whether the receiver understood your message by asking for feedback. Ask the receiver to explain what he or she thinks you said. When you listen to others, provide feedback. Tell them in your words what you understood them to say or ask for an example of what they meant.

6. Use visual aids. Whenever possible, put what you have to say in writing. Use graphs and pictures to support your meaning. When information is sent on multiple channels, the receiver has a better chance of decoding the message as you intended.

7. Be careful with your nonverbals. With the exception of the smile, all nonverbal signs are culturally defined. For example, in the United States, communicators who feel fond of each other are very likely to point their feet at one another. In many parts of the Middle East, pointing your feet at people communicates the opposite—that you have no respect for them. At all times you must keep your feet under you and away from others.

Technology

New communication technology is being developed every day. The most remarkable thing about communication technology is how fast we are "putting it to work." Word processing, electronic mail, voice mail, fax, conference calls, video conferences, desktop publishing, and computerized graphics are as common in organizations today as the electric typewriter and the dictation machine were fifteen years ago.

Unfortunately for communicators, we have accepted all this new technology without really understanding the effects it might have on how we communicate. In the 1960s, Marshall McLuhan demonstrated that communication technology has an impact on what we communicate and how we process, or think about, communications. We are just beginning to investigate the influences of these modern technologies. Some of the most recent findings indicate that shorter messages (one computer screen) are more effective than longer ones. The modern communicator must become an expert at writing abstracts.

Because typeset-quality print is widely available, our expectations for the appearance of letters and reports have risen. Software that checks spelling and grammar has decreased the reader's tolerance for errors in editing. Of course, spell checkers do not find *is* when you meant *in* nor do they find that *not* has been left out of a sentence. So although the reader's tolerance for errors has decreased, the writer's responsibility for careful proofreading has not.

Easy-to-use graphics programs have increased the number and quality of visual aids communicators expect. Both written and verbal presentations are expected to have professional visual support.

The Team Environment

More and more businesses are moving toward organizational structures that incorporate teams, committees, quality circles, and other problem-solving groups. These new structures require that managers and workers take a more collaborative and less competitive approach to communication. The modern manager must be more interactive. Rather than sitting in an office, reading and writing reports, today's manager is working actively with others. Developing your interpersonal communication skills, especially good listening skills and conflict resolution skills, will allow you to get the most out of the groups you work with.

Legal and Ethical Considerations

The reality of life in the United States in the 1990s is that government and the courts have a significant impact on our everyday decisions. Modern communicators need to guard against legal charges of defamation—the charge that you have made false and malicious statements about someone. Letters of recommendation and performance review are especially vulnerable to such charges if their result is to get someone fired or to keep someone from getting a job or a promotion. Concrete language and reference to specific instances will help protect the business communicator from charges of defamation.

Invasion of privacy is another legal and ethical topic important to business communicators. People at different levels of the organizational hierarchy will interpret messages differently. A manager may ask an employee about what arrangements he or she makes for child care out of a general interest in the employee. However, if the employee feels vulnerable, he or she may believe the question is an invasion of privacy—the manager has asked a question irrelevant to the employee's ability to perform the work.

Other invasion-of-privacy issues arise when organizations keep files on employees and allow a variety of individuals access to the files. For example, should an organization be able to keep records of the medical claims an employee makes against company-provided health insurance? What if the claim is for drug-addiction therapy? How about AIDS-related claims?

An Approach to Excellent Communication

All of the above leads to the conclusion that communication in the information age requires new skills. *Planning* is an important part of effective management. Planning your communications is perhaps the most important planning a manager can do. The following questions aid in communication planning:

1. What is your goal?
2. What do you know about the receiver of your communication?
3. What is your receiver's most likely response to your message going to be?
4. What communication competencies can you bring to this situation?
5. How can you reduce both your and the receiver's anxiety?

These questions will be addressed in greater detail in the remainder of this book.

An effective communicator accurately transfers the meaning he or she has in mind to the mind of the receiver and is equally adept at understanding what receivers are communicating back. Physical, psychological, social and structural barriers can get in the way. The English language itself encourages certain perceptual biases: polarization and static tendency.

Communicators can do much to improve their communication skills. They can control the connotation of their messages by reducing the number of highly emotional words they use. They can reduce their level of abstraction by choosing more concrete words. They can use nonverbal communication to support what their words say. In general, they can take greater responsibility for the quality of their communication. When a miscommunication occurs, they can consider how they contributed to the faulty transfer of meaning. The ability to communicate effectively is the essential managerial skill and thus deserves all the attention we can give it.

2

Audience and Adaptation

Communication can be intrapersonal—when we talk to ourselves—or interpersonal—when we exchange messages and meanings with others. Whenever we take on the difficult challenge of transferring meaning to others, it is critical that we understand the receivers of our message.

In this chapter, we investigate the important role that the receiver plays in effective communication. The same message transmitted to different audiences may need to be rephrased or sent by a different channel. Effective communicators adapt to their audience.

INTERPERSONAL ROLES

Without question, the most important concept in this book is "audience adaptation." When you communicate with someone, especially in writing, you are probably doing so to solve a problem—yours or your receiver's. The fastest way to do that is to adapt or **adjust your style and organization** to fit the receiver's needs and expectations.

If you wrote to a scholarship committee asking for a grant to assist you to complete your education, you would write differently than if you were writing to your family asking them to help you pay for your schooling. Notice how even in writing about the two situations I've used different language and created a different tone—"to assist you to complete your education" versus "to help you pay for your schooling." Almost everything in your letters would be different. Your words, punctuation, organization, and even format would be adapted to suit your audience. In some situations, we make these changes easily and without conscious thought. Sometimes, however, communicators forget whom they are communicating with, and the results are less effective than they could be. In all cases, thinking about your audience before you begin writing or speaking will improve the communication.

This observation holds true because you play different roles with different audiences. Different audiences have different expectations of you. You do not walk into your boss's home and open the refrigerator, although you might do that at your best friend's house. One professor may expect students to ask questions in class and to offer examples of the day's lesson and may call on them by name if they do not offer to speak up. Another professor is displeased when students "interrupt" the flow of a lecture by asking questions.

Most people easily adjust their behavior to suit the roles they are assuming. When you perceive that your audience has more authority or status than you, you behave more formally. When you know that your audience has a particular expectation of you, you will probably try to meet it, even if it requires of you a behavior you do not usually use.

Assume you are not fond of sweets and you are trying to cut back on fats. As a result, you rarely eat desserts. However, if your grandmother offers you a chocolate-chip cookie which she "made especially for you," you will probably have one. Unless your audience repeatedly expects you to do things you find uncomfortable, you will probably be accommodating. Adjusting your behavior to the roles you play is seen as a sign of interpersonal competence.

AUDIENCE

A first step in determining your proper role in relationship to others is to think carefully about the others and to note consciously what you know about them. You cannot compose useful or convincing information until you know who the audience is. Many students have never given audience much thought because for fifteen or more years, their audience was a consistent one—the teacher. Teachers know more than students about the subject being taught, have higher hierarchical status, are older, are in an evaluative position, and have many other similar student-teacher relationships. Once the student adjusts for personality differences, most aspects of the student role remain constant.

In business communication, you will be writing to many different audiences. And each different audience may require a slightly different approach, a different language level, or a different level of formality.

Think carefully and specifically about your reader. What is he or she like? How formal? How educated? How knowledgeable about this topic? How busy? How conservative? How funny? To organize your thinking about your audience, you might use a standard journalist's approach to investigating a story. Answer the questions *who? what? where? when? why?* and *how?* Here's an example of a helpful audience analysis. Let's assume that our job is to write to the purchasing department and request a special order of supplies which we need by next Wednesday at the latest.

Who is my reader?

Eljin Wenno, director of materials and purchasing. He has been with the company for seventeen years and in this position for six years. He is conservative; some in the company would say he's old-fashioned. He likes to have everything documented in writing. He works slowly but carefully.

What does my reader know about the subject?

He really knows very little about our new product. He has helped us get parts for it before, but he has never understood why we are trying to get the product to market so fast.

Where is my reader in the organizational hierarchy?

Two levels above me. He reports directly to the vice president of operations.

When will my reader get my memo?

Because this is a rush order, I'll need to deliver the letter today even though I know that Tuesdays are the best day for him because they are the slowest.

Why is this reader important to me and my goal?

All rush orders have to be approved by him, although he does not need to do the paperwork himself, nor would he have to find suppliers since I can provide that information.

How much information does my reader need?

He needs to see that I have considered several suppliers and that I have evidence to support the one I recommend. He also needs the specifications exactly and completely written out. He will probably expect a precise breakdown of the costs.

Every audience analysis needs to include the question *What is my audience's most likely response to my message?* Use your best empathetic skills to imagine what your reader's most likely response to your message will be. In other words, try to imagine that you are your reader. Will your reader be delighted to hear what you have to say? Or will he or she have a neutral response? Perhaps your reader will be angry or disappointed with your message. Or will your reader have a guarded "Why should I do that?" response? Your answer to this question about your reader will assist you in choosing the most appropriate/effective message strategy to use. We will discuss message strategies in chapters 6–9. In our example, the director of materials and purchasing will not be very happy to get our request.

This example shows how audience analysis can be an effective step in planning any communication. The answers to the questions begin to suggest certain topics that must be included if we are to solve our problem.

Unknown Readers

When you are writing to a reader you do not know, you will need to *imagine* the reader—pretend you can see the reader and imagine the answers to the questions. You can start this process by thinking about the kind of job your reader has and whether you know others who have similar jobs. That will give you a sense of how busy the person is, the kinds of things that assist that person in doing his or her work, and perhaps something of the person's education and experience.

Primary and Secondary Readers

An additional level of difficulty in audience analysis arises when your letter is going to several readers. Frequently we send a copy of our letter to others who might need or want the information. In the case of the supplies purchasing, we might want to give the engineer in charge of developing the new product a copy of the memo to the director of materials and purchasing. That would accomplish two things. It would allow the engineer to check the accuracy of the specifications, and it would let the engineer know that the parts have been requested. The director of materials and purchasing is the primary reader, and the project engineer is the secondary reader. To some degree, both readers need to be considered.

Sometimes we have *unintended* secondary readers. Memos get passed around organizations. The press sometimes gets hold of internal reports. Subordinates end up with copies of confidential performance evaluations. Employees read the board of directors' request that the President resign quietly. The savvy organizational communicator always considers unintended secondary audiences as well as intended ones.

Identifying the reader and his or her needs is essential to adapting the message to the audience. You will be more successful if you will actually **write down** what you know about your reader. That will help you keep a mental image of him or her (or them) before you as you write.

ADAPTATION

Once you have a good idea of your audience, you can use different elements of language style and structure to adapt your message. Let's use an example so we can identify the elements. Suppose you would like to have a special Friday off work so you can attend a dear friend's wedding. In the first adaptation, your boss is a very formal, "follow the rules" person. In your day-to-day work, you rarely see him. When you do, he seems to be busy, thinking about something else. Here's the request you might send to him:

Example 2.1

Dear Mr. Singleton:

The major order we are preparing for Scarsdale Corp. must be shipped by Thursday, June 14. Everyone on the shop floor is giving this project top priority. Their quality is excellent, and we appear to be right on schedule with production.

The user's manuals and warranty information must also be completed by June 14. Usually that project is completed under subcontract to W.R.I.T.E. Corp. Their union has threatened to strike, so it seems prudent to establish a contingency plan. With your approval, I will personally prepare the documents. In order to remain on schedule with shop-floor production, this work will be completed in the evenings. Rather than overtime pay, I would prefer to take compensating time off.

Once the order is shipped on Thursday, June 14, I would like permission to leave work. A close friend is being married on Friday, June 15, and I would appreciate the opportunity to attend.

Please initial at the bottom if this plan meets with your approval.

Sincerely,

Now let's assume your boss is a warm and friendly person. You work side by side on many projects, so you've come to know one another pretty well. You respect his knowledge and wisdom, and he seems to appreciate your dedication and energy. Here's the letter you might prepare for him:

Example 2.2

Dear Ted:

The Scarsdale project is coming along great. The guys on the shop floor are really putting their hearts into this one. They're turning out top quality work. They'll have no problem meeting the shipping deadline.

Usually we have the user's info prepared by W.R.I.T.E. Corp. I suppose you've heard they are likely to go on strike this week. How about I take charge of that? I'm confident I can keep everything on target at work *and* get some new experience if I do the manuals in the evenings.

In exchange, I'd appreciate your giving me Friday, June 15, off. Remember my roommate from college? That lucky character is getting married then, and I would love to go. Let me know what you think.

Thanks,

Tone

These two examples differ in tone. **Tone is the emotional content of written language.** In a face-to-face conversation, we express our emotions with our voice quality and body language. In writing, our emotions are just as clearly expressed using style and structure. As a writer who wants to adapt messages to audiences, you will need to gain a conscious awareness of how tone is created in writing. Most people would say that the first example was more formal than the second. The important question is what makes them come to that conclusion?

WORD CHOICE

In Chapter 1 we discussed the large number of words in English. Over its history, English has borrowed from several major languages. It is this rich borrowing and when the borrowing took place that make word choice a significant part of tone and formality. Old English was largely a Germanic language. The Angles, Jutes, and Saxons, all Germanic, settled in Angle Land, now England. Their language, Anglo-Saxon, became the base for English. Anglo-Saxon words tend to be short, frequently one syllable. Many of the words children learn first are from the Anglo-Saxon. Examples include *lid, cup, cold, want, help,* and *word,* as well as those words we refer to as "four-letter words."

In the 500s and 600s, Christianity was brought to England. With it came many Latin words. Words that refer to religion, such as *spirit, religion, regent, redemption,* and *evolve* and many other words like *infect* and *information* were added to the language.

In 1066, William the Conqueror invaded England from Normandy and took control of the government and the church. Many members of the upper class in England learned Norman French because they wanted influence and power. The use of French words became fashionable. Examples of words with French roots include *sanitary, routine, machine,* and *management.* Words borrowed from the Latin and French are called Romance-Latinate.

As a result of this history, when we want our tone to be formal or we want to impress someone with our power and influence, we use the multiple-syllable Romance-Latinate words. When we want our tone to be informal and friendly, we use more of the single-syllable words from the Anglo-Saxon background. *School* is informal; *education* is formal. *Truth* is informal; *veracity* is formal. *Talk* is informal; *verbalize* is formal. *Hurt* and *heal* are Anglo-Saxon; *poisonous* and *venomous* are Romance-Latinate.

PRONOUNS

In general, formal writing has fewer pronouns than informal writing. In formal writing, when we want to refer to something several times, we choose a synonym rather than a pronoun. For example, in the opening paragraphs of the letters to the bosses, the more formal example refers to the work as an "order," a "project," and "production." The more informal letter refers to the same thing as a "project," "work," and the pronoun "one." Very formal writing never uses the word *I* to refer to the writer. Instead, the writer is referred to in the third person as *the author*. Other personal pronouns are used sparingly. Informal writing, on the other hand, tends to use many personal pronouns. In the letter examples, the second letter uses twice as many personal pronouns as the first.

SENTENCE LENGTH

Informal writing uses shorter sentences. Shorter sentences are usually more readable; however, their structure cannot be varied as much as that of a longer sentence. In our example letters, the first averages just over fourteen words per sentence; the second, more informal letter averages just over ten words per sentence.

CONTRACTIONS

A contraction is a word which reflects the fact that when we speak, we don't make all the sounds—we contract some of them. In speaking, we would say "Since I can't meet you, I'll be home at two" rather than "Since I cannot meet you, I will be home at two." *Can't* and *I'll* are contractions (the apostrophe indicates to the reader that some letters have been omitted). Abbreviations like *info* for *information* are a different form of contraction. Informal writing more closely reflects conversational speech, so it frequently uses contractions. The more formal the writing, the less likely a writer would be to use contractions.

STRUCTURE

The more formal the writing, the more likely it will have a well-organized structure. When you write a note to a friend, it is likely to wander some in its logic. Effective communication principles encourage all writers in all situations to get in control of their logical structure; however, the longer and more formal the piece of writing, the more important that is.

Content

Adapting to the audience may mean *what* you say may change as well as *how* you say it. In the example of arranging for a Friday off, something you know about a boss may encourage you to approach the situation completely differently. Suppose your boss knew the young person being married and had also been invited to the wedding. In such a case, the content of the request would change. You might write something like the following:

Example 2.3

> Dear Ted:
>
> What great news about Chris's wedding! Would you like to drive there together?
>
> Of course, both of us out on a Friday will require some planning. I know I can get the Scarsdale Project out on that Thursday. Is there anything else you would like me to be responsible for? To celebrate Chris's new life, I'm happy to make myself available every evening between now and then. Just let me know what needs to get done.
>
> Sincerely,

In this case, your knowledge of the audience includes additional information about what your reader knows about your subject. You can use that information to adapt not only the style and tone but also the content.

Thinking about who your audience is and what he or she expects from you will help you assume an effective relational role. Once you understand your role with your receiver, you can adapt or change your message so it can most easily be accepted and understood by your audience.

Adaptation can be accomplished by changing the tone or emotional content of your writing. Word choice, style, sentence length, content and structure will all change as you adapt your message to your audience.

EXERCISES

Exercise 2.1

Write two thank-you notes; one to a family member saying thank you for some item or favor, the other to a work or school colleague saying thank you for some item or favor. Compare the two notes for style and tone.

3

Making the Receiver Central to the Message

Once you have thought about what you want to communicate and your audience, you can prepare a draft of your message. You are more likely to achieve a positive communication outcome if you write from the reader's point of view.

Although the idea is a simple one, many writers have difficulty with it. Writing from the reader's point of view means thinking about your message not as the sender, but as the receiver. If you received your message, how would you most like to have it organized? What phrasing would you find most sensible?

In this chapter, we will discuss how to develop messages that involve the reader—that make the receiver central to the message.

SELF-INTEREST DOES NOT EQUAL SELF-CENTERED

Whether or not we like to believe it, most of us are exceedingly self-centered. We see others and their behavior only in relationship to ourselves. When we are cranky with a subordinate, we know our short temper has much more to do with the pressures we're under and the lack of rest we've had than with the subordinate's behavior. When our boss is short-tempered with us, we worry we have done something to cause it. Whether we are assuming the active or the passive role in a relationship, we tend to see ourselves as central—as the critical element.

You can use this observation about people to improve your communications with them. When you want to solve problems, make your audience central to your message. Rather than talking about what you want, talk about what your receiver wants. In so doing, you will get more of what you want. Customers are more likely to buy your product if you tell them what the product can do for *them* rather than how much commission *you* will receive if they buy it.

Making the reader central to your message is "you-attitude." Next to audience analysis and adaptation, it is the most important way to improve the effectiveness of your communications. This idea is so important to improving your interpersonal communication skills that we will devote an entire chapter to it.

Since we are prone to making ourselves central to any communication, letting go of that tendency and making the reader central may be especially challenging. The results will make the effort worthwhile.

Examples

Let's look at some examples. We'll start with some extreme cases and once we have a clear idea of what you-attitude is, we'll work toward more refined examples. Here's an obviously self-centered example:

Example 3.1A

I was hoping to get some information on your company for a report I'm writing in one of my classes. The professor wants me to use current information, so asking you seemed like the surest way to get it. I hope you'll send a copy of your most recent annual report right away because I got started on this project late, and I'm getting desperate.

A more reader-oriented version:

Example 3.1B

Would you please send me a copy of your latest annual report. Your company's rapid growth is serving as an example to students in management at Dartmouth. You can teach us a great deal about how to manage effectively. Thank you very much for your assistance.

Here's another unfortunate writer-centered example:

Example 3.2A

We here at Kolin Paperworks appreciate your order. Unfortunately, our shipping supervisor has been out ill all week, so we are having trouble keeping up. We've added overtime help at significant cost to us, so we will have your order sent to you by Thursday at the latest.

Making the reader central to the message would result in a rewrite like this:

Example 3.2B

Thank you for your order. You can expect shipment on or before Thursday.

These examples demonstrate how a message can be flipped from the writer's viewpoint to the reader's viewpoint. Rather than focusing on what you want, try to see your problem, idea, or solution as the reader would see it.

TOOLS FOR "YOU-ATTITUDE" WRITING

Becoming a reader-centered writer poses several challenges to the writer. As with any change, you must first see or take note of the goal. Then you can begin to change your behavior so that it matches the goal. Most people first change their behavior mechanically, using a variety of prescribed behaviors. Once they are used to the different specific behaviors, the changes become more a matter of attitude, more automatic and graceful. Let's begin with some mechanical approaches for improving your you-attitude.

Substitute You for I

Writers can mechanically improve the you-attitude of their writing by reducing the number of *I, we, my, me* and *our* pronouns and increasing the number of *you* and *your* pronouns. Here are some examples of this approach:

Example 3.3

I've asked Bill to call you.	Bill will be giving you a call.
I would like to reserve a room at Claremont Resort for Monday, May 23.	Please reserve a room for me May 23.
I'm tired of always having to tell you where I'll be.	You won't always be able to reach me.
I hope you will be able to come to a party on May 23.	Please come to a party on May 23.

I appreciate the way the house looks.	Thank you for cleaning the house.

When you observe yourself using too many first-person references, try to flip the sentence around so it is about the receiver rather than about the sender.

Use You or Your Before I, Me, or My

Another mechanical approach to improving your you-attitude is to make sure you use *you* or *your* **before** you use *I, me* or *my*. In other words, **never** start a letter with *I*. Habit might tempt you to begin a letter with "I'm writing to ask for your help with this year's United Way campaign." A major problem with that type of beginning is that it puts the sender in the most important part of the sentence—at the beginning, as the subject of the sentence. All the grammatical and positional emphasis is on the sender. The you-attitude writer will make the *receiver* the subject of the first sentence—perhaps something like this: "Your generous contribution to last year's United Way campaign made it possible to send twelve inner-city children to summer camp, where they learned important interpersonal and computer skills." Rather than beginning "I want," begin "Would you please." Instead of "My company appreciates your business," begin "Your business is important."

Apply the Empathy Index

Another mechanical approach you can take to making your writing more reader-centered is to apply an empathy index to your messages. Count all the times you refer to yourself or your company in any communication. Then count all the times you refer to the receiver or the receiver's company. Make certain you have more receiver-focused references.

Check for Grammatical Emphasis

In English, every sentence has at the minimum a subject and a verb. Most sentences also have an object—the thing upon which the action takes place. Longer sentences have adjectives and adverbs that qualify the subject, object, and verb. For example, "Mike ran." is a simple sentence with a subject, "Mike," and a verb, "ran." "Mike ran home as fast as he could." adds more information but does not change the fact that "Mike" is still the subject of the sentence. The grammatical emphasis is on Mike. You can make your writing more receiver-centered if you make the receiver the subject of most of your sentences. It is possible to apply the empathy index and have more receiver-focused references than sender references. However, if the sender references serve as subjects in your sentences while the receiver references are always serving as objects, your writing will not be very you-attitude. Here are some examples.

Example 3.4

I would prefer it if you were to meet with your group in the morning.

Your answer is not the one I was looking for.
If you send the check by Thursday, I will deduct 2% from your bill.

Once again, work on flipping your sentences around so that the receiver holds the important grammatical role of subject.

CHANGE YOUR PERSPECTIVE

Behind mechanically replacing sentences that talk about *I* with sentences that use *you* is an **attitude**—a mind-set. It involves seeing situations from the reader's point of view rather than your own. Look at each situation from the receiver's point of view and write from that perspective. For example, "I was delighted to meet you Saturday" includes as much you-attitude as "You were delightful on Saturday." If you just mechanically change all your sentences, you are likely to produce very awkward writing. **The goal is to change the tone or attitude behind your writing.** Here are some examples of you-attitude which result from imagining what it would be like to be the receiver of the message.

Example 3.5

The order was shipped Monday.	You will have your order by Wednesday.
We make our molded plastic products using only the finest quality resins.	Your customers will be able to tell the quality of these plastic products.
Our insurance rates have been rated lowest in the state by AAA.	According to an AAA survey, you save money on your insurance with us.
The president must receive all bid proposals by 5:00 p.m. Wednesday.	Submit your bid proposal to the president by 5:00 p.m. Wednesday.
The employee shall include in his gross income the amounts received under such contract.	As the employee, you must include as gross income any money you receive under this contract.
Those persons who are sensitive to pollens are encouraged to avoid leaving their windows open at night.	If you suffer from pollen allergies, close your windows at night.

You-attitude makes your writing more interesting to the reader. Research indicates that people are receiving less and less of their information from writing. If you want your readers to get information or help you solve a problem that requires them to read, make the reading as interesting as possible to them.

Example 3.6A

> The relationship you create with your readers depends on the language you use to address their needs or interests.

By using *you* twice and *your* once in the previous sentence, I am addressing you, the person reading this material. But consider this revision:

Example 3.6B

> Writers create a relationship with readers by using language that addresses their readers' needs and interests.

Notice how the revision creates a distance between you and the material. You're no longer involved directly. Instead, you're reading an impersonal statement. Many older textbooks are written in the impersonal style. Without any conscious observation, students know which books are written in an impersonal style because they fall asleep reading them. Business communicators want their readers to be awake and engaged. That's why you-attitude writing is so important.

See situations from the readers' point of view. Write with them in mind. Make them central to your message.

*P*eople *see themselves as central in their system of relationships. You are more likely to achieve positive communication outcomes if you write from the reader's point of view.*

You-attitude is a mind-set. To be effective at communicating using you-attitude, imagine the concerns and expectations of your audience. You-attitude involves seeing situations from the reader's point of view rather than your own. Once the reader's concerns have been identified, make the reader central to your message. Use you *and* your, *make the reader the subject of most of your sentences, and apply the empathy index.*

EXERCISES

Exercise 3.1

Rewrite the following sentences, making them more receiver-centered:

I have made a reservation for you at the Hilton Hotel for Thursday, March 6.

My company would like you to join us for an open house to celebrate our fifth anniversary of business.

With your approval, I would like to leave early on Friday, October 14.

If I am going to approve your application for a student loan, I will need your signature on this form.

I'm counting on your making Tuesday's meeting.

All employees are expected to attend the training workshops.

Writers can make writing more interesting by making it more reader-centered.

Students find dorm life both frustrating and beneficial.

I was wondering if you would be willing to help me decorate for the anniversary celebration.

I would like to get some information from you about the population and weather of your town.

4

Principles of Communication

This *chapter introduces several principles of communication. The word*
principle implies that these observations underlie, or are basic to, all com-
munication. Mastering communication principles will take you a long way
toward mastering all forms of communicating with others. These principles
will help you improve your communication face-to-face, on the telephone,
in formal writing, and in informal writing. The message strategies pre-
sented in Chapters 6–8 are based on these principles.

The principles addressed in this chapter include positive phrasing,
position of emphasis, message length, and active and passive voice.

In addition to these principles, this chapter discusses the importance of
clarity, correctness, completeness, conciseness, confidence, and conversa-
tional tone. Applying these six ideas will improve the degree to which your
audience understands your message.

POSITIVE PHRASING

Many of the situations we face in life are neither inherently bad nor
inherently good. The degree of stress we feel and the good-bad labels we
attach to situations are largely a matter of choice. For example, losing your
house and belongings to fire would usually be labeled as bad and would

result in feelings of pain, loss, and fear. However, in retrospect, some victims of home fires are grateful that they were forced to clean house and start over fresh. The fire allowed them the freedom to let go of old baggage, of wornout memories, of reminders of painful pasts. When we choose to look at situations and apply positive labels to them, we are said to be optimists. **Optimists** expect favorable outcomes. **Pessimists** expect unfavorable outcomes.

Medical research provides significant evidence that looking at the world optimistically is good for your health. Optimists go to the hospital less frequently than pessimists and stay in the hospital for significantly shorter times when they do go. They are more likely to be successful in their careers, achieving goals more rapidly.

Even if you are not ready to accept optimism as your way of looking at the world, as the bias through which you perceive things, phrasing your communications with others positively is more likely to result in positive communication outcomes—for both you and those you are communicating with. Whether you are in a positive mood or a negative mood, you would probably rather have lunch with someone who is positive. Whether you had a good day or a bad day, you would probably rather go home to someone who is in a good mood. As it turns out, so would everyone else. The result is the principle of *positive phrasing:*

People prefer positives.

Focus on the Positive

Nearly everything that can be said negatively can be turned around and phrased positively. "Thank you for your trouble" becomes "Thank you for your help." "I can't make the meeting Thursday" can be phrased "I already have a commitment on Thursday." "We do not give plant tours on Saturday" is more positively phrased "We give plant tours every Monday through Friday at 10:30." In general, the approach is to focus on what you **can** do rather than what you cannot do.

Avoid Words with Negative Connotations

Some words, in and of themselves, have strongly negative connotations. Generally you will want to be wary of these words because they invoke unpleasant thoughts in the listener. Examples of such words are *mistake, problem, error, damage, loss,* and *failure.* Words that deny, such as *no, do not, can not, refuse,* and *stop* fall in this category. And some words have unpleasant effects, to at least some readers, just by the way they sound and the mental pictures they invoke: *guts, grime, sticky, bloody, gummy, soggy.*

Here are two examples of negative phrasing changed to positive phrasing.

Example 4.1

The negative approach:

We regret to inform you that we cannot permit you to use our conference facilities for your meeting. We have already made a commitment to the Hospital Auxiliary for that day. We can, however, let you use the boardroom at the headquarters building. The problems with that suggestion are that the board room seats only 40 and parking is more difficult.

A positive rephrasing:

The conference facilities are being used by the Hospital Auxiliary that day. Would the boardroom at the headquarters building work for you? It seats 40.

Example 4.2

The negative approach:

We received your letter in which you claim that we are responsible for the damaged condition of three cases of Nooketoh dinnerware. We can assure you that we regret the problems this has caused you. Even though we believe that the problem was most likely caused by negligence on the part of your shipping personnel, we shall assume the blame and replace the damaged cases.

A positive rephrasing:

Three cases of Nooketoh dinnerware are on their way to you. You should have them by Thursday.

POSITION OF EMPHASIS

In every communication, there are two especially important moments— the beginning and the end. The receiver of a message lets information that is delivered first and last *count more* as he or she decodes the message. The first and last information receives greater emphasis. This observation holds true whether the communication is written, spoken, or nonverbal.

The Beginning

The beginning is important because it "sets the tone." When the beginning of a communication is positive, the communicators are likely to anticipate that the rest of the communication will be positive. As a result, they set up a self-fulfilling prophecy. They selectively perceive data that support their expectation. On the other hand, if the beginning is negative and full of friction, the communicators will begin selectively perceiving data that support the expectation of a poor outcome.

When you call a friend on the telephone, you can frequently tell how the conversation will go based only on your friend's "hello." There are cheerful hellos, short-tempered hellos, cautious hellos, and tired hellos. Once you hear that first word, you set your expectations. You might even decide to talk about something other than your original reason for calling.

The beginning of any communication speaks loudly—it is a position of emphasis.

The End

The end of a communication is also a position of emphasis. Readers (and listeners) remember best what they hear last. All the research on information processing indicates we can process only a limited amount of information. We are most likely to remember, and make judgments about, the most recent information we have. In the context of a letter or conversation, the most recent information is the information that comes last. For example, research indicates that readers of direct-mail newsletters from stores are most likely to read and remember the first sentence and any postscript (P.S.). As a result, excellent communicators take extra care with what they say first and what they say last. They apply the principle of *position of emphasis*.

Receivers pay more attention to first and last information.

Example 4.3

Wasting the positions of emphasis:

Dear Betty:

I just wanted to write you a brief note to say thank you for the lovely luncheon. Your house looked beautiful and the food was heavenly. How you can entertain the way you do while working full time is beyond me.

Well, I have seventeen things to do this afternoon, so I'd better make this short. I look forward to seeing you again soon.

Using the positions of emphasis effectively:

Dear Betty:

Thank you so much for the lovely luncheon. Your house looked beautiful and the food was heavenly. You make it all look so easy. As a result, your guests can really relax.

I appreciate our time together. You are a very special person.

Example 4.4

Wasting the positions of emphasis:

Dear Mr. Kadee:

Per your request, enclosed please find our remittance of $234. This is to serve as reimbursement for your covered loss re. the use of your vehicle.

The body shop's service writer indicated that your automobile would be ready no later than Thursday. We will process the remainder of your claim as soon as they notify us of completion.

Using the positions of emphasis effectively:

Dear Mr. Kadee:

Here is a check for $234. This will reimburse you for the rental car costs.

We will pay for the body work just as soon as the body shop bills us. The service writer says your car will be ready by Thursday or perhaps earlier.

GOOD NEWS GOES IN THE POSITIONS OF EMPHASIS

Combining the principles that "people prefer positives" and "first and last are positions of emphasis," we arrive at another communication principle.

Put good news in the positions of emphasis.

Dealing with Good News

Obviously, when you have good news to transmit, this principle indicates that you should address it immediately. Put the best news at the very beginning.

If you have bad news to transmit, put it in the middle of the message. That way you have time to prepare your reader for bad news, and you have the important ending position to reestablish rapport and goodwill.

Because bad news seems to consume more of our psychic attention, many communication experts suggest that for every piece of bad news you must convey, you should convey four pieces of good news. That leads them to conclude that bad news should be presented like this:

> Good news
> Good news
> Bad news
> Good news
> Good news

THE SHORTER THE MESSAGE, THE GREATER THE PUNCH

In general, it is better to keep both your words and your sentences short. As we discussed in Chapter 2, our classic *business English* grew out of a sense that "fancy" language was more impressive and powerful than simple, straightforward language. Fancy word choice, combined with

Victorian England's sense of manners, resulted in a business letter that was very long and flowery with many "humbly beg"s and "your honored servant"s.

Long ago we began to find the language in a Dickens novel old-fashioned. Author Rudolf Flesch would like us to use "sport-shirt and blue jeans" language in our business writing. His advice is to keep your average sentence length 11–14 words. The *Wall Street Journal* encourages its staff writers to average nine words per sentence.

Words carry meaning. The fewer you use, the more meaning each carries. When we write long sentences and combine them into long paragraphs, the work each individual word does becomes smaller. Here are some examples.

Example 4.5

Thank you.

Your helpful assistance during my hospital stay was greatly appreciated by both me and my entire family.

Help!

If you have any available time this weekend, I could certainly use your able assistance in getting my household goods moved to my new apartment.

Combining this principle with our understanding that people prefer good news to bad, if we are communicating something positive, we can use short, punchy language. When we must tell someone "no," we might want to lengthen our sentences, effectively "padding" the bad news with extra words.

ACTIVE VOICE "HITS HARDER" THAN PASSIVE VOICE

In active voice, the doer of an action is the subject of the sentence: "Joe Montana *threw* twenty-three passes in the first quarter." We can picture the quarterback looking down the football field, finding his receiver, and *throwing* the ball.

In passive voice, the actual doer of the action becomes the object of the sentence: "Twenty-three passes were thrown in the first quarter by Joe Montana." In fact, in passive voice, the doer of the action can be completely dropped from the end of the sentence: "Twenty-three passes were thrown."

Active voice draws attention to the doer; passive voice takes attention from the doer. As a result, when we want to say something good, we can use active voice. When our message is unpleasant, passive voice will reduce blame and take attention from the doer. Here are some examples.

Example 4.6

Active voice:

Gary sells over $100,000 worth of televisions each month.
Colleen arrived in time to hear the plane fly over.
You will receive your order by Saturday.

Passive voice:

An accounting error was made. (by Jeffrey)
A loss in profits was reported. (by the president)
The headquarters building was broken into. (by the burglar)

THE SIX Cs OF COMPETENT WRITING

Some important writing advice can be more easily remembered if it is grouped as a set of six Cs. These important contributions to competent writing include clarity, completeness, conciseness, correctness, confidence, and conversational tone.

Clarity

Writing takes time and money. Some companies estimate the average business letter costs about $16 when the writer's time, the typist's time, and the stationery and postage are figured in. Obviously it is in everyone's best interest to write effectively the first time. Improving the clarity of your writing will go a long way toward effective communication.

ORGANIZATION

Clarity is affected by a number of writing characteristics. Probably the most important is the overall structure of your message. Have you presented your ideas in a logical way? Time you spend organizing your message before you begin writing will save both you and your reader significant time later. The traditional outline is one method for organizing ideas. Another method is called a decision tree. The trunk is the outcome you seek—the decision you want your reader to reach. The major branches are the major points you will need to make in order for your reader to reach the decision. The message is filled out by smaller supporting branches—ideas, examples, or evidence. Figure 4.1 provides an example of a decision tree. You might try using one to help you organize your ideas. A decision tree

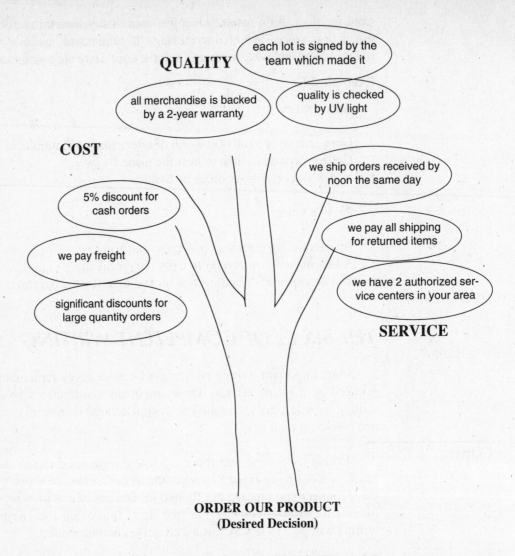

QUALITY

each lot is signed by the
team which made it

all merchandise is backed
by a 2-year warranty

quality is checked
by UV light

COST

we ship orders received by
noon the same day

5% discount for
cash orders

we pay all shipping
for returned items

we pay freight

we have 2 authorized ser-
vice centers in your area

significant discounts for
large quantity orders

SERVICE

ORDER OUR PRODUCT
(Desired Decision)

Figure 4.1: Example of a Decision Tree

makes it easy to organize your ideas as you think of them, no matter in what order you think of them.

You can also improve your organizational clarity by presenting your ideas in an order the reader will perceive as logical. If you are talking about historical events, arrange your ideas from the least recent to the most recent. For example, if you want to ask for an explanation of your current phone bill, you might relate what you know of the history: "I arranged for service to become effective on August 15. I received my first bill on

September 3. That bill included a $35 installation charge. On October 5, I received my second bill which included a $17 installation charge."

If you are presenting ideas that have a physical reality, discuss them in a spatial arrangement. For example, if you are discussing plans with an architect, you might relate your concerns as if you were walking through the room: "The entry should be covered because winter storms often come from that direction. Just inside, the floor will need to handle the water from umbrellas and wet shoes. We were hoping you could design a section somewhere in the main hall which would receive enough light for large plants, maybe even some flowering ones."

WORD CHOICE

Remember to think about who your audience is and what he or she knows. That will help you choose effective words. If your reader shares your background, you can comfortably use jargon—the words and phrases common to a particular subgroup. For example, a professional pilot would know that the moist adiabatic lapse rate varies with temperature. If your audience does not consist of professional pilots, however, you may need to explain that you are discussing a method for determining how stable or unstable weather patterns are at different altitudes.

As mentioned in Chapter 1, your writing will be clearer if you choose more concrete and less abstract words. *Saturday* is more concrete than *sometime this weekend. Three* is more concrete than *a few.*

In summary, you can improve the clarity of your writing in the following ways:

- Structure logically and coherently; keep sentences and paragraphs short.
- Use vivid language; avoid jargon and obtuse, abstract words.
- Use a language level appropriate to your audience and objective.

Completeness

When you communicate to solve problems, include enough information so the receiver of your message can help you. For example, if you want to reserve a hotel room, the reservationist will need to know the dates you want to reserve. The example may seem silly—certainly anyone writing for a reservation would include that most important piece of information. However, any reservation clerk can tell you that not everyone does. Another example comes from corporate personnel departments. They commonly receive résumés which do not include the candidate's address and phone number. Effective communicators put themselves in their receiver's shoes and ask if all the necessary information has been included.

Have you ever been invited to a party and wondered what you should wear? Had the person doing the inviting thought about the situation from the receiver's point of view, information about appropriate dress would have been included. In summary, you can improve the clarity of your communication by the following:

- Put yourself in the reader's position.
- Give complete information (*who, what, where, when, why, and how*).

Conciseness

Conciseness means being succinct—expressing much in few words. It is not the opposite of completeness. The excellent writer is both complete and concise. A grandiose or pseudolegalistic style with long sentences and clever flourishes looks pompous and pretentious, not professional. The professional writer delivers all the information and saves the receiver time in the process.

Some writers forget that words have meaning, so they become redundant. They say the same thing several times. Here are some examples of redundant phrases and their more concise alternatives.

Example 4.6

In the future years to come	In the future
Estimated at about	Estimated at
Consensus of opinion	Consensus
Needless to say	(substitute nothing)
My personal opinion	My opinion
Due to the fact that	Because
In view of the fact that	Since
Until such time as	When

Editing is a critical step in the process of writing concisely. Look for words that add little meaning and remove them. For example, fewer than one half of *that*s are necessary to the meaning of the sentence. If they add nothing, remove them. All forms of the verb *to be* (*is, was, were, had been, will be*, etc.) are less lively and concise than more active verbs. Any time you can remove them, do so. If you are writing in the past tense, using the simple past will result in the most interesting language. Interestingly, many past-tense verbs can be changed to present tense without changing meaning. Here are some examples showing wordy and edited alternatives.

Example 4.7

The apple that he gave to Paul was very sweet.
The apple he gave Paul was very sweet.

The conversation that was going on in the next room held special interest for Beth.

The conversation in the next room held special interest for Beth.

Thursday had been the very most taxing day that Juan had experienced the entire month.

Thursday was the most taxing day Juan experienced all month.

Usually companies find that their workers have more accidents on Mondays than on any other day of the week.

Companies find their workers suffer more accidents on Mondays.

I'll need to have copies of the first draft to be sent to each of the vice presidents.

Please send a copy of the draft to each vice president.

In summary, you can make your writing more concise by doing the following:

- Don't overkill; say it once, say it simply.
- Remove redundancy. *Now* can substitute nicely for *at this point in time*.
- Edit. Simplify past-tense verbs. Remove *to be* verb forms. Delete *that* when it adds no meaning.

Correctness

When information is inaccurate, at best it makes understanding difficult, and at worst it results in lost time, money, and productivity. The effective communicator strives for correctness. Check your facts. Proofread addresses and numbers carefully. Use standard business format. Strive for what the quality-control experts refer to as zero defect. Your goal is not "good" or "better," but *perfection*.

Let me tell you about a student of mine and his problem with correctness. He was applying to the major accounting firms for an entry-level accounting position. He had shown his résumé to his father, a professor, and several friends. They had made some suggestions for improvement, which he incorporated in the final product. He typed his job application letters, included a copy of his résumé, and mailed his applications. As he was tidying his desk, he took one last look at his résumé, because he was so proud of it. It was then he noticed his job objective read: "To obtain a position as a pubic accountant." Correctness not only saves time and money; it saves significant personal embarrassment! Work on zero defect correctness. Have colleagues help you. Sometimes we see what we expect to see rather than what is actually on the page. Friends can help you proofread.

Secretaries can help you proofread. However, any error they miss remains your responsibility.

Computer technology is having an interesting impact on our perception of writing correctness. Word-processing programs typically include spelling checkers. Many include grammar checkers. As a result, our tolerance for errors and typos is decreasing. The problem is that spelling checkers pick up only misspelled words—they do not identify properly spelled words improperly substituted for other properly spelled words, like *form* when *from* was intended or *is* when *in* was intended. The conclusion, once again: the writer is responsible for correctness.

In summary, you can improve the correctness of your writing by applying the following advice:

• Check grammar, spelling, and punctuation.
• Use appropriate format and good-quality paper.
• Check the accuracy of your information (price, address).

Confidence

The modern business writer writes from a position of knowledge and expertise. As a result, his or her writing reflects a sense of confidence. As mentioned in Chapter 2, business writers no longer take a position of deference to their readers. They write as equals—partners in the transaction of business. Their tone reflects their sense of confidence. How can writers convey a sense of confidence? Avoid equivocating language. Equivocating language questions itself. Here are some examples, followed by more assertive and confident examples.

Example 4.8

I hope we can meet Tuesday at 2:00.
Let's meet Tuesday at 2:00.

Perhaps the best solution would be to leave in separate cars.
Let's take separate cars.

Would it be all right for me to arrive a half-hour late?
I regret that I must arrive a half-hour late.

I humbly beg to differ.
I disagree.

Begging your pardon . . .
Excuse me . . .

A confident tone is achieved as a result of real confidence. When a writer actually feels insecure, the tone is likely to become overbearing when the writer strives for a sense of confidence. For example, writers of job application letters sometimes end their letters too strongly. Rather than confidently asking for an interview—"May we arrange an interview to discuss my qualifications for the position"—they overbearingly demand one—"Please call to arrange an interview to discuss how you might use my talents." The most direct path to confident tone is through real confidence: Research your facts. Think about your message and your audience. Realize that clear, direct communication is appreciated by the receiver. Keep the receiver's needs clearly in mind. In summary, a confident tone can be achieved by applying the following suggestions:

- Be assertive but not overbearing.
- Use emphatic rather than wishy-washy language.
- Make your statement of purpose clear and simple.
- Use tact.

Conversational Tone

Modern business communication strives for a conversational tone. As Rudolf Flesch says in his book *Say What You Mean*, use shirtsleeve and blue-jean language. The best letters are written as we would talk in everyday language. You have not only the right but perhaps the responsibility to be friendly in business communication. Some business writers believe that in order to be "professional," they have to be cold, legalistic, and distanced from their audience. That is definitely an old-fashioned approach to business communication. Talk on paper. Have conversations with your readers. Imagine they are sitting across the desk from you and you are solving your problems cooperatively.

Because of our history of using formal, semilegal language in business writing, we may believe that is professional. Actually, the most professional language is language which solves problems with the least expenditure of energy. Taking a friendly approach to our reader reduces his or her resistance. Throughout the world, people are more comfortable doing business with people they know—with friends. When we use our correspondence to establish friendships, we improve our business relationships.

CONTRACTIONS

In Chapter 1, we noted that contractions like *you'll* and *aren't* are typical of informal writing. Because they reflect the way we speak, they are also more conversational. Unless you know your reader will dislike your doing so, use contractions in your writing.

DANGLING PREPOSITIONS

In formal English, we are taught not to end a sentence with a preposition. The preposition is supposed to go before the object of the preposition. For example, formal English requires us to write "In which department did you receive the most training?" Conversational English frequently has the preposition dangling at the end of the sentence: "Which movie did you go to?" Once again, unless you know your reader will dislike your doing so, placing the preposition at the end of the sentence will make it sound more conversational.

PERSONAL PRONOUNS

Formal English uses very few personal pronouns. The language becomes distanced and impersonal because people are referred to by title, job, or function—"Managers are responsible for the safety of their subordinates." Conversational language personalizes the message—"As a manager, you are responsible for the safety of your subordinates." Using personal pronouns and writing directly to an individual will make your writing more conversational.

Some business writers forget that they are writing to real people when they write to large companies like IBM or AT&T. Conversational tone improves when you remember that a real person with hopes, dreams, and perhaps headaches will open your letter, read it, and try to help you solve your problem. Treat your reader with respect. Try to have an interpersonal conversation. In summary, your conversational tone will improve when you apply the following:

- Develop clear, specific images of readers.
- Write as if you were talking.
- Edit for flow, clarity, syntax, and structure.
- Be polite, including *please* and *thank you*.

TONE

Remember that in writing as well as speaking, words have both connotative and denotative meaning—they gain meaning in addition to their dictionary meaning from the order in which they appear and the number you use. Tone, or emotional content, is as important in writing as it is in speaking. The reader can "hear" your feelings and attitudes. As Edward Goldfinger, in *A Better Way of Writing* (South-Western, 1987) says,

Love your subject. It's difficult to get your reader involved if you yourself have little passion for your subject. The more involved you are with a topic, the easier it will be to write about it, and the easier it will be for your reader to read about it. When a person is truly enthused about a topic, words flow easily. When you feel passionately, it is easy to speak with passion.

What about those situations where you do not love the subject? The best alternative would be to find someone who does to write the letter. If that won't work, try to find something about the situation or the writing challenge which you can love.

Love your reader. In this situation, love means respect, acknowledge, and accept. When there's love between writer and reader, information and ideas can flow freely, without friction or loss of power. For real communication to take place, it is essential. If you cannot approach your communication situations with a sense of respect and acceptance for your reader, then you are better off not communicating. Many people write when they are angry. The sensible ones throw their letters away. The foolish ones mail them.

Write when you're feeling good. This may not always be possible, but you'll be surprised what a difference it makes. When we're happy inside, we naturally perform better. We're also more understanding of others— and more giving. This is important, because when we write, we need to be giving—not only giving of correct and useful information, but also giving in a personal sense—for example, by showing concern for the reader's welfare. When we're feeling good, it's easier to choose words that will help the reader to feel good. And a reader who feels good will be more inclined to read, understand, and act on what we've written.

Overall, Goldfinger's observation is that the key to successful writing lies in creating harmony with your reader.

RETAINING GOODWILL

Goodwill is all the value a company has accrued because of its relationships with its customers, suppliers, and community. Retaining goodwill is the most important outcome of effective business communication. Study after study indicates it is significantly cheaper to retain a customer you already have than to attract a new customer. Studies also show that a satisfied customer is likely to tell three people about the experience. A dissatisfied customer is likely to tell four or five times that many. So in all business communication, no matter what other goals you have for the messages you send, your primary goal must always be to retain goodwill.

Suppose a customer refuses to pay you for a job you completed. The law and common sense will tell you you have a right to be paid and that you should take every legal means to see that you are paid. The principle of retaining goodwill may require you to think about the situation differently. Certainly you should apply everything you know about excellent communication skills in an attempt to encourage your customer to pay. Beyond that, the costs in terms of lost goodwill may be too high.

For reasons no one seems able to explain satisfactorily, the world is surprisingly small. With over four billion people on the planet, logic would suggest you could easily lose yourself in the crowd. The fact is, you come across the same people over and over again in your life. You take a summer trip to the Panama Canal, and beside you at the locks is the person who lived across the street from you seven years ago.

A student friend of mine was about to graduate and wanted nothing as much as to work and live in New York City. He applied to several companies and received an interview with a downtown Manhattan company. He flew to New York, spent the night in a hotel, and in the morning caught the subway to the corporate offices. Unfortunately, he was a little late and had to run to catch the subways, barely making it on the train before the doors closed. In the process of jumping aboard, he knocked into an older man. In his nervousness, he said, "Why don't you get out of the way, you old coot." Of course, the old coot turned out to be the personnel manager. No matter what the situation, the most effective communicators remember the world is remarkably small. They do not burn their bridges. They retain goodwill.

*T*he letters we write can spell the difference between making and missing an important sale, landing and losing a job, a yes or a no. Applying the principles of communication improves your odds of achieving your goals.

The principles of communication suggest that in all cases, whether you're writing or talking, certain observations hold true: people prefer positively phrased communication over negatively phrased communication; people are most likely to remember what they hear first and last; the fewer words you use, the more impact each has; and active voice is more interesting and compelling than passive voice.

Effective writing is clear, complete, concise, correct, confident, and conversational. Effective communication establishes a relationship between the sender and the receiver that, above all, retains goodwill.

EXERCISES

Exercise 4.1

Rewrite the following sentences so they are positively phrased. Remember to focus on what you can do rather than what you cannot do.

1. Unfortunately, none of our operators is available to take your call at this time.

2. Although we do not believe the damage was caused by faulty material or workmanship, we will repair your toaster under warranty.

3. Smoking is not permitted anywhere except in the employee break room.

4. You failed to provide the dimensions of the living-room window, so we are unable to complete your curtains.

5. We cannot deliver your order until Friday.

Exercise 4.2

Change the following sentences from passive to active voice. You may need to add information.

1. The newspapers were delivered before the morning board meeting.
2. Frequently, accounting errors are identified by auditors.
3. The most significant pass of the game was caught by Jerry Rice in the last minute of the third quarter.
4. The top-salesperson award was given to Christine Hsu by CEO Jackie Mackelroy.
5. Management's interpretation of the contract was contested by the labor council at Tuesday's general meeting.

Exercise 4.3

Rewrite the following sentences, changing them from active voice to passive voice.

1. The National Motor Club chose Washington, D. C. for its fifth annual meeting.
2. Beebee closed the deal by offering to deliver the computer on Saturday.
3. Consumers favor greater product variety.
4. The university is seeking donations for its library fund.
5. James Brown will present his concert live at the Coliseum.

5

Memo and Letter Conventions

In addition to the words you choose for conveying your message, you also send a nonverbal message. The nonverbal message arises from three characteristics of letters and memorandums, all under your control—paper, typeface, and format. Before a reader reads the first word of your letter or report, you have sent a strong nonverbal message. The reader begins to form an opinion about the quality of your work just by looking at and touching it.

In this chapter, you will find a discussion of the nonverbal elements of written business communication and some examples of the standard business-letter and memorandum formats.

THE NONVERBALS OF WRITTEN COMMUNICATION

When you communicate face-to-face, some of the message comes from your words and the order in which you put them. However, research indicates that as little as 7 percent of your message may come from your words. The rest of the message comes from nonword elements in your message. Some of those are voiced—that is, your speaking rate, volume, and tone convey a portion of your meaning. The largest part of your message is nonverbal. It comes from what you're wearing, how you're standing, how much eye contact you're making, and so on. Even when you communicate in writing, you communicate nonverbally.

Paper

Stationery can have a significant impact on your message. Good-quality stationery feels heavy—should be 20–24 lb. bond. It has a certain color. Business writers usually choose white, ivory, or light gray. Other light colors can be used in certain situations. For example, Mary Kay Cosmetics uses a light pink paper, which promotes the company's feminine image. Standard business stationery is 8 1/2 x 11 inches. Half-sheet paper (5 1/2 x 8 1/2 inches) is called executive stationery and is used for goodwill notes, frequently handwritten.

Stationery also has a surface texture called finish. Standard types include: classic laid, linen, flannel, and kokle. Usually stationery has a design called a watermark that is observable when the paper is held up to the light. The message should be typed so that the watermark is right side up. Sometimes the watermark is the logo of the company that made the paper; however, larger companies sometimes have their own company logo for the watermark.

Type

Three elements of the type have a nonverbal impact on the receiver of a written message. The first is the darkness and clarity of the type. Worn ribbons and poor-quality copies transmit a sloppy message. If the type is so light that the reader must struggle to see the message, the reader is more likely to be short-tempered and impatient with the writer. Change your printer ribbon frequently and keep the keys of impact printers and typewriters clean.

A second element is the font—the design of the letters. Some type fonts are very plain; the letters have no decoration, or "tails." These fonts belong to the *sans serif* family. The following are examples of *sans serif* typefaces.

Helvetica   Avant garde   Optima

The other large grouping of type fonts are called *serif*—the letters in these type fonts have decorations, or "tails." The following are examples of *serif* types.

Bookman   New Aster   Times Roman

Some fonts are easier to read than others; some look more professional, and others are used for special effect. Some examples of special-effect fonts are shown on the next page.

Freestyle Script   *Zapf Chancery*   **COTTONWOOD**

In general, *serif* fonts are easier to read. Every font has a character, a mood. Every font communicates a slightly different nonverbal message. As you read letters, become aware of what the type font communicates to you and choose a font which is readable and looks neat and professional.

By choosing different fonts for different occasions, you can nonverbally support your message. Once the writer has chosen a font, most word processors allow the entire font family to be used. This manual is written in Helvetica, 12-point size. The following are adaptations of Helvetica:

Bold   *Italics*   larger size (14 pt.)   smaller size (9 pt.)

THE PARTS OF A LETTER

Over the years, letter writers have reached general agreement on the parts of a letter. Following the definition of each part, some models are included that show how the different parts are used and where they go in the letter.

Dateline

In the United States, the conventional form for typing the date is month, day, and year (February 14, 1988). Europeans and U.S. military personnel are likely to switch the order to day, month, and year (14 February 1988). Abbreviated date forms such as 2/14/88 are considered too informal for typed letters and memos.

Return Address

Whenever you use a printed letterhead, the return address is already there. When you are writing a personal business letter, you will need to type your full address, single spaced, directly above the date. Usually envelopes are discarded, so you must include your address in case a reply is necessary. Although the company name is typed above the address, the writer's name is not. It appears at the bottom of the letter, just under the signature.

Inside Address

The mailing address of the person you are writing to, including the complete title and name of the person addressed, must be included on the letter. Obviously the receiver knows his or her address. The inside address is for your benefit. When you keep a copy of the letter, it will have all the information.

Subject Line

A subject line allows both the sender and receiver to identify quickly the subject of the correspondence. The subject line tells what the letter is about. It may also allow the writer to refer to a particular case number or invoice number without using the important beginning sentence to do so. For example, a subject line might be "Purchase Order #34244; Oct. 12, 1993."

Salutation

The salutation is the "Hello there" part of the letter. We almost always begin our letters *Dear*. If you know the receiver well or if the situation is informal, the salutation may be by first name—"Dear Elisabeth." However, most business situations call for the last name preceded by an appropriate title—"Dear Dr. Hemingway."

People are funny about their names. They *always* notice if you have spelled them correctly. As a result, it is important to determine your receiver's name and use it.

If you do not know and cannot find the name of the person to whom you are sending your letter, use a position title. We seem not to mind being called by our position titles. Doctors are frequently called "Doc," students greet their teachers by calling out "Hi, Teach." *Mom* and *Dad* are actually position titles. Many employees refer to their bosses as "Boss." So if you do not know your receiver's name, the salutation may be "Dear Customer Service Representative" or "Dear Public Relations Officer."

The traditional courtesy title for men is *Mr.* Historically, females were given one of two titles—*Miss* for an unmarried woman and *Mrs.* for a married woman. Because the marital status of males is not signified by the Mr. title, many have argued for a similar marital-state neutral courtesy title for women—*Ms.* Many large companies, IBM for example, have a company policy to use Ms. for all correspondence with women. The only time when you would not want to use Ms. for women is if you know a particular woman has a preference for some other title. You would know that because she would put her preferred title in parentheses following her typed name.

Complimentary Close

The complimentary close got its name because it used to be a compliment to the reader. An example of an old-style close: "Finding myself in many ways deeply in your debt, I close with humble reverence." Today, the most widely used close is *Sincerely*. The second most widely used close is *Truly*.

Mixed, Open, or Closed Punctuation

Different degrees of punctuation can be used following the introductory and closing parts of a letter. **Mixed** punctuation means that a colon is used after the salutation and a comma is used after the complimentary close. **Open** punctuation means that no punctuation follows either the salutation or the complimentary close. Either of these punctuation styles is appropriate in the United States. When you write internationally, you may wish to use the **Closed** punctuation style. Each line in the return address and inside address is followed by a comma. The complimentary close is followed by a period. In this situation, the complimentary close is usually longer, approaching a full sentence in length and style.

Signature Block

The signature block consists of two parts: the sender's handwritten signature, and following that, the sender's name or name and title, typed. Handwriting analysis is a field most of us know little about. A lack of professional training, however, does not stop us from making judgments about people based on their signatures. A tiny, scratchy signature leaves a different nonverbal impression from a large, rounded signature. To a significant degree, your signature is under your control. Look at your signature and try to imagine what impression others are forming about you. If you want them to reach a different conclusion, develop a different signature.

Informational Notations

In the lower left corner of the letter may appear a variety of abbreviated notations. These all provide additional information to the receiver of the letter. For example, *Encl.* is a common abbreviation for *enclosure* which means something is being sent along with the letter. Sometimes the specific enclosures are listed.

Example 5.1

Encl.   Map of city
Demographic info sheet
Copy of employment contract

Another common notation is *cc*, which stands for "carbon copy." Whenever you send a copy of the letter to someone other than the official receiver of the letter, it is polite for you to let the receiver know that others have read this letter. Today most people send photocopies rather than carbon copies, but the *cc* remains. The names of those receiving copies are included.

Example 5.2

cc   Melvin Markowitz, Dean
Judy Minton, Chair
Abe Bradley, Committee Chair

Another common informational notation is a set of capital letters followed by a slash and a set of lowercase letters. The capital letters are the initials of the sender, and the lowercase letters are the initials of the typist (EFB/vb). This notation began as a method of quality control. The production of typists could be determined by counting the number of letters they typed in a day.

Postscript

A postscript (P.S.) is a bit of writing that comes after any notations. *Postscript* means "after the writing." It is rarely used in business writing because it looks like an afterthought—as if the writer were not completely organized when the letter was written. There is an exception to this observation. More and more writers of sales messages use a postscript because the postscript is in the last or ending position of emphasis. The marketer can put catchy information in the P.S. and thus hold the reader's attention at the very end of the letter.

Second-Page Heading

Most business letters are complete on one page. Some companies even insist that their employees stick to a single page. However, when the length of a letter must exceed one page, the following page or pages must be labeled for quick identification. About one inch down from the top, type the name of the person to whom the letter is addressed, the date, and the page number. Use only plain paper (no letterhead) for your second and following pages. The paper should match the letterhead paper exactly.

Drop down about one inch below your page heading and begin typing. When you have reached the end of your message, you are ready for the signature block. In other words, do not attempt to center your writing vertically.

Although most letters contain most of these parts, different formats may place them in different places. The situation also determines which of the parts will be included. For example, if you plan to include a map with your letter, you would include an abbreviated notation for an enclosure. If you aren't including anything with your letter, you will have no need for the enclosure notation.

STANDARD FORMATS

There may be many ways to include all the necessary information in your letter; however, there are only a few *standard* formats. Because business readers are used to certain formats, you will be perceived as professional if you follow one of them and unprofessional if you don't. Each of the format examples which follow is standard. You may use any one that pleases you; however, don't mix the formats. In the last chapter, we discussed the importance of correctness. Using a standard format is one element of correctness.

An Example of
Full-Block
Letter Format

6435 Alpine Way
Carlile, OR 97934
February 16, 1991

(This is the letter writer's address, the "return address")

(This is the date the letter was written; avoid abbreviations like 2/16/91)

Mr. Jason Bascale
Wages and Benefits Dept.
Cascade Lumber Corp.
789 S. W. Regal Ave.
Fossil, ID 99621

(Use a title with the name of the person who will receive the letter)

(This is the receiver's address; the "inside address")

Subject: Full-Block Style

(This is a subject line. Not all letters include this information.)

Dear Mr. Bascale:

(This is the "salutation." Use a colon in business letters)

You are receiving a letter written in the full block letter format. Notice that every line begins flush with the left margin. Not only are the return address and inside address typed even with the left margin; so are each of the lines in the body of the letter.

You will notice that each paragraph is single-spaced. To indicate to the reader that a new paragraph has begun, there is a double space between paragraphs.

Even the closing and signature are flush to the left. This particular format is fast and easy to type because no indenting is required.

Sincerely,

(This is the "complimentary close")
(Leave four spaces here for the signature)

Christine Sanders
encl

(Type the sender's name)
(If you include something with your letter, indicate that)

cc Harry Downs

(If you send copies of the letter to others, list their names)

Sid Levine

An Example of Modified-Block Letter Format

(The return address and date are typed starting halfway across the page)

Butler Building Corp.
555 North Ave.
Durham, NC 40423
March 22, 1991

Ms. Darlene Wong, Manager
Advertising Administration
GNC Inc.
4 Providence Drive
Waldren, CA 95333

(The inside address is typed flush left)

Dear Ms. Wong:

Most business letters begin each line of a paragraph at the left margin. If you believe your letter would look better if you indented the first word of a paragraph five spaces, you may do so with this letter format.

The only differences between modified block and full block are the placements of the return address and date and the complimentary close and signature. In modified block, these start halfway across the page. Everything else is along the left margin (unless you want to indent the first word of each paragraph).

Of course, if you have some special points you want to emphasize, you may set those off by indenting. This method of making points clear is appropriate in any letter, memo, or report format. For example, the following are things you might indent:

1. Questions you want the reader to answer.

2. Procedures you want the reader to follow.

3. Items you want the reader to send you.

When you include a list of items, make the grammatical structure of each element in the list the same. Called parallelism, this helps your reader to understand you easily.

Very truly yours,

Juan Gonzales
Director of Communications

*An Example of
Full-Block
Letter Format
When You
Have a
Letterhead*

The BeadWorks Corporation
1173 Second Avenue
New York, New York 10021
(212) 555-0247

June 20, 1991

Dr. Michele Corrigan

Suite 520

Rio Lindo Avenue

San Raphael, CA 90143

Dear Michele:

Notice that even when you receive a relatively informal letter from a friend, if your friend writes to you on a business letterhead, the salutation is followed by a colon. The only time to use a comma is when you are hand writing the letter.

When your company has a letterhead, the design often determines whether you use full block or modified block. If the visual "weight" of the letterhead is on the right, use full block. If the visual "weight" of the letterhead is on the left, use modified block. If the letterhead is centered, either format will look good. Choose the one you like.

Sometimes on the line after the typed name of the person sending the letter you see initials which look like this: GW/vab. These are the initials of the person who dictated the letter (in capitals) and the person who typed the letter (in lowercase letters.) These allow companies to keep performance information on typists in the typing pool.

Regards,   (Even when George signs only his first name,
                             his full name is typed below)

George Whitehead
GW/vab

An Example of Administrative Management Society (AMS) Simplified Format with Letterhead

MISSISSIPPI DELTA COMMERCIAL DEVELOPMENT
"LAND USE MANAGEMENT SPECIALISTS"
121212 SOUTH UNION DRIVE
NEW SOUTHPORT, MS 24545

November 14, 1993

Ms. Pauline Smythe, Vice President

Smith, Smythe, and Jones

514 S. W. 41st Street

Portland, OR 98803

EXAMPLE OF AMS SIMPLIFIED STYLE

Promoted by the Administrative Management Society, an organization of secretaries and first-line managers, this letter format is the most modern. It is highly recommended by many and strongly resisted by others. Notice, Ms. Smythe, that this format has no salutation. The letter just begins.

The subject line, which is always included, is in capital letters and is not preceded by the word *subject.* Most writers try to include the receiver's name in the first paragraph, although that is not a requirement of the format.

As with the full-block style, all lines begin flush with the left margin.

The final interesting difference between AMS Simplified and other letter formats is there is no complimentary close. The letter simply ends with the letter content. It is signed as usual.

Gregory Jackson
Personnel Manager

An Example of Memo Format

M E M O R A N D U M

(type this word in all capitals leaving a space between each letter)

Date: September 22, 1993   (type "Date:", tab, and the date)

To: Dr. Lyle Littleton, Dean   (type "To:", tab, and receiver's name, title, dept.)
College of Theater Arts

Dr. Hali Ahmad, Dean   (memoranda are frequently sent to more
College of Engineering   than one person. List all receivers)

Dr. Kathleen Hall, Assoc. Dean
Student Affairs

From: Dr. Elaine Wong, Dean*EW*   (type "From:", tab, and sender's name, title, dept.
College of Education   Rather than signing a memo at the bottom, initial it
here)

Subject: Homecoming Events   (type "Subject:", tab, and a clear title that summarizes the content)

The key difference between a memorandum and a letter is the format. Memorandum format is used when you write to someone *in your company*. Use letter format when writing to someone not in your company. The way you approach your topic should depend on your audience and your message, not on whether the receiver is in your company or outside the company. In other words, the text of the message will be organized by applying the message strategy most appropriate in the situation.

As with full-block letter format, do not indent the first line of a paragraph. Instead, single-space within paragraphs and double-space between paragraphs.

When your letter or memorandum is longer than one page, begin the following pages by typing the receiver's name, the date, and the page number at the top of the page. For example, this memo would begin "Drs. Littleton, Ahmad, and Hall, September 22, 1993, page 2." Then drop down three lines and resume typing your text.

Memorandums are quite different from letters in two ways. You don't sign a memo at the bottom; rather you initial it after your name on the "From:" line. And when you send the same message to several people, you may send them copies rather than a retyped original as you would with a letter. Make a checkmark near the name of the person who is receiving this particular copy.

ENVELOPES, ADDRESSES, AND FOLDING

A sloppily folded letter carries the marks of its poor start with it forever. A well-folded letter is easy to read and may even unconsciously surprise and delight the reader. If you are using the larger "business size" or No. 10 envelope, folding your letter neatly is easy. Fold the bottom third of the letter up. You might try to use the bottom of the page to "underline" the receiver's name. Doing so will draw subtle attention to the receiver's name and to the beginning of your message. Fold the top one-third of your page down and insert it in the envelope so that the letter is ready to read as soon as it is removed—no turning or looking for the beginning.

If you must use a small evelope, first fold your letter neatly in half. Then fold the bottom third up and the top third down.

Your letter's nonverbal elements begin communicating before the reader has read any of your written message. For some, putting the words on paper is such a chore, they may forget the power of a letter's nonverbals. However, all the nonverbal qualities of your letter are under your control. Remember to pay attention to them.

The quality of the paper you use, for your envelope and your stationery, is noticed by receivers. The clarity and darkness of your type affects the ease with which a reader can read your message. The format you use will either support the conclusion that you are a business professional or lead the receiver to question your competence. Effective business communicators keep the nonverbals of their communications in mind.

6

Positive and Routine Situations

Different communication situations call for different communication strategies. In the next four chapters, we will discuss the four main strategies or approaches to effective communication. Having a strategy helps you develop confidence and improve the speed with which you prepare your written business communication. To some degree these strategies also work effectively for spoken communication.

In this chapter, you will learn an effective message strategy to use when your message is positive and/or routine.

DIRECT MESSAGE STRATEGY

Most (about 80%) of the letters and memos you will write during your career will be to an audience who will be glad to hear what you have to say (or will at least consider your message to be neutral). Before you begin to write your letter, ask yourself how your reader is likely to respond to your message. If you believe the audience will have a **neutral or positive** response to your message, then the **Direct Message Strategy** is the appropriate strategy to use.

The principles of communication suggested that when you have good news to deliver, you deliver it immediately. Those principles are applied in the direct message strategy. In the direct message strategy, you begin in the very beginning by stating your reason for writing.

Direct Strategy Situations

Some situations where you are most likely to use this strategy:

- thanking, congratulating, apologizing, wishing well (good will situations)
- ordering, confirming, acknowledging
- requesting information
- requesting routine claims and adjustments
- responding positively to a request or claim

In all these situations, the reader will either be glad to get your letter (for example, when you are ordering something or when you are telling someone something positive—You got the job!) or will at least consider your message typical business (for example when you request that a product be repaired during the warranty period). Later in this chapter we will discuss each of these situations individually.

General Advice

Some general advice to use with this type of strategy:

- Emphasize goodwill.
- Get to the point by beginning directly.
- Ask specific questions.
- Use lists to organize information.

As we discussed earlier, every business-communication situation is a goodwill situation. That holds especially true when you have only good news to report. Building goodwill is an important part of direct-message-strategy letters.

The Strategy

I. Use an immediate beginning.

If you are writing to request information, ask for it in the first sentence. If you are writing to thank someone, thank her in the first sentence. If you are telling someone he got the job, say so right away. Remember that *first* is a position of emphasis. Put the good news at the beginning.

The immediate-beginning directive is difficult for some people. They have trouble just starting right out. Here are some examples of slow beginnings that walk around the topic and waste the position of emphasis. They also confuse the reader, who is likely to be asking mentally "Why are you telling me this?"

Example 6.1A

In my financial analysis class, we have to write a term paper on the importance of annual reports to the investment decision.

I am considering moving to Greensboro because I have been offered a job there that sounds promising.

Your catalog of special products which support wetlands conservation was in my mailbox this week.

Here are more direct beginnings for these situations. They make clear why the letter was written—what the writer wants. The middle of the letter provides plenty of opportunity for adding explanation.

Example 6.1B

Please send me a copy of your current annual report.

Would you please send me information on the city of Greensboro and its surrounding area?

Please send me the following products from your winter catalog.

If you believe these direct beginnings are too abrupt, put yourself in the reader's position. Suppose you work for the Greensboro Chamber of Commerce. Knowing right away that the writer of a letter wants information about the city will allow you to listen more carefully to clues in the rest of the letter about what information would be most helpful. When the writer starts with some discussion about job offers, you have no idea why the writer is telling you that.

II. Additional information.

Use the middle paragraphs of your letter to supply information you think the reader might need. If you are placing an order, use the middle of the letter to list the product information. If you are requesting information, use the middle of the letter to explain why you need the information and specifically what information you need. If you are writing a goodwill letter, use the middle paragraphs to expand your thanks or congratulations.

To make this part of your letter clear and well organized, consider using lists, indenting your points, or numbering your questions. When a writer includes a number of questions in narrative form, the reader may overlook one or more of them. Or the reader may be unable to tell whether they are separate questions or a single question expanded. Using lists and setting off the different points with numbers or bullets makes your writing clearer and helps the reader follow you. (A "bullet" is a dot •, triangle ▲, star *, etc. that draws attention to the points you are making.)

Here are some examples of questions that have been poorly stated. Their organization makes reading more difficult.

Example 6.2A

I would especially like to know how your company responded to the economic slowdown of the late 1980s, early 1990s. Did you downsize at all, or did your business and strategy remain about the same? How did your industry perform overall? In other words, was your industry hit particularly hard by the larger economy, or did it do well by comparison? That information would make a difference in evaluating the quality of the responses taken by your firm.

Example 6.3A

I've heard from friends that Greensboro is very pretty, but I'm wondering if that means it rains there a lot. I like spending time outdoors—camping, fishing, hiking, and that sort of thing. Also, I won't have enough money to buy a house for two or three years, so I'll need to rent. I was wondering what the rental market is like.

Several things are wrong with these approaches to asking for information. The questions are not well organized to make it easy for the reader to provide the information the writer wants. Also, these examples are very writer-centered. Indeed, the employee at the chamber of commerce will be able to provide more helpful information if he or she knows something about the writer. On the other hand, much of the information in these two examples is simply the writer focusing on personal issues without any thought about the reader and the reader's needs. Here are some better examples which allow the reader to help the writer faster and more accurately.

Example 6.2B

• Has your company changed its strategy in the last four years? If so, is that discussed in your annual reports? If not, how might an investor learn about your strategic changes? If you have any additional information on your strategy, I would appreciate having a copy.

• Does your annual report discuss how well your company has done compared to your industry as a whole? If not, I would also appreciate any information you could supply on that topic.

Example 6.3B

• Please include information on the weather in Greensboro during July, August, September, and October. I am especially interested in the high and low temperatures as well as the normal rainfall for these four months.

- Do you have any information on the availability and typical costs of two-bedroom rentals? If not, would you please include names and phone numbers for your local papers.

Notice how much clearer the grouped formatting makes the questions. It allows any necessary explanation to be included with the specific question to which it refers. Notice also that the improved examples have omitted the I-attitude information except for what is specifically necessary to the reader.

When requesting information, some writers leave room after each question so the reader can answer right on the letter and return it. That saves time and paper in certain situations. The reply-on-this-letter approach is used more frequently within a company than when a writer is writing to someone in another company.

III. Forward-looking goodwill close.

Use the last paragraph to build goodwill and talk about the future. For example, "I look forward to working with you on the High Dam project" or "The conference should be an exciting one. I look forward to seeing you there." Your goal is to indicate that you see the relationship between you and the reader continuing in the future. Try to make your closing specific to the specific reader and situation. In other words, **do not** use a general form-letter closing like "I look forward to doing business with you in the future" or "Thank you for your consideration." Once an expression has been used and overused, it becomes at best unseen and at worst an irritant. When "Have a nice day!" was first used, it sounded sincere and caring. Now it sounds phony and uncaring. Keep that in mind when you write your goodwill closing. The end of a message is a position of emphasis. You will waste it if you end your letters with a worn-out, automatic platitude.

Here are two effective closings for the Greensboro Chamber of Commerce letter, one very personable, the other somewhat more formal.

Example 6.4

Thank you for your help in my decision-making process. If Greensboro is as nice as my friends say it is, I look forward to thanking you in person one day soon.

Thank you for all the information on Greensboro. I look forward to receiving it.

In summary, to write effective Direct Strategy letters,
- Begin directly.
- Stick to the point.

- Give all the details in a well-organized way.
- Close courteously.

Although all good-news and routine-news situations are best treated following the direct message strategy, each specific situation type has its own special challenges and opportunities. In this section, you will find some additional advice.

As you get more and more comfortable with writing business letters, you may begin looking for opportunities to practice your new skills. Goodwill situations offer an endless number of these. Excellent communicators actively seek out goodwill situations so they can make positive contact with others. They acknowledge others and the accomplishments of others. They share the good times and in so doing make them seem larger and last longer.

Goodwill letters can be typed on regular stationery, can be typed on half-size executive stationery, or can be handwritten. Many businesspeople keep a supply of blank-inside greeting cards in their desks so they are always prepared to send a goodwill message.

THANK YOU

Thanking people for time, things, information, and orders builds goodwill. In the thank-you letter, say "Thank you" first. Then provide additional information about what was given. Close with a goodwill, forward-looking close. Here's an example of a thank-you letter:

Example 6.5

Thank you for the lovely sweater you sent for my birthday.

How sweet you are to remember that blue is my favorite color. I also really appreciate the machine-washable nature of the yarn.

I can't wait to show you how nice the sweater looks on me. I look forward to seeing you during my trip to Nebraska in October.

CONGRATULATIONS

Often people do things they are proud of, yet nobody notices. You can easily build goodwill by telling people you noticed their accomplishments. A congratulations letter says "Congratulations" in the first sentence. It then expands on the good news and closes with a forward-looking close. Here's an example of a congratulations letter:

Example 6.6

Congratulations! You must be very proud of graduating.

You certainly worked hard to accomplish this goal. It isn't easy to keep up with your studies while you also support yourself and do a competent job at work.

Be sure to send me your new address once you get settled in Portland.

SYMPATHY LETTERS

Although it may not seem so to the writer, a letter to someone who has experienced the death of a loved one requires the direct message strategy. The receiver wants to hear from you and wants to hear what you have to say, so begin directly by expressing your sympathy. Say you're sorry. If you knew the person who died, in the middle of your letter mention something you remember of the person—especially something kind or funny. If you did not know the deceased, make an offer of support to your friend. The more genuine the offer, the better. Close with good wishes for the future. Here's an example of a sympathy letter:

Example 6.7

I was so sorry to hear about your loss.

Lizzie is irreplaceable in our hearts. I can't think of her without thinking about "Carry our bags to Baghdad, Dad" or "How would you like to fall in there with one hand tied behind your back?" or "He could break a moose's back with one fell swoop of his mighty paw!" What a character. . . and what fun she shared with us all.

I hope you are getting on OK. I think of you often and wish you the strength of heart to accept the unacceptable. I'm here if I can be of any help to you.

The reality of life is that the older you get, the more frequently you will be called upon to write sympathy letters. It is part of business etiquette and personal etiquette. Remember that these letters serve a beneficial purpose and are positive messages. That might make it easier for you to write them.

Ordering, Confirming, Achnowledging Letters

Most ordering is done using a standard order form, a fax, or the telephone. However, sometimes you need to order by letter. For example, suppose you heard an author discuss her latest book on the radio, and you want to get a copy. You can use direct message strategy to order. Especially when you are ordering more than one item, arrange the product information logically, making the quantity, description, and price clear. Include shipping instructions, your delivery address, and either a check or charging instructions.

If someone has ordered something from you, it is helpful to send a letter of confirmation, especially if she ordered by phone. Then everyone has a written record of the transaction. Confirmation letters are also used when one company accepts the bid proposal of another company. Here is an example of a letter where a contractor accepts a subcontractor's bid:

Example 6.8

Your bid for completing the electrical work at 2724 Downing is accepted. All the terms and conditions you set forth in your bid proposal are acceptable. You can expect a check for $45,000, one-third of the contract amount, by Friday.

To review the main points:

1. Total contract price is $135,000.
2. Work is to begin no later than Monday, June 3.
3. Work is to be completed no later than Monday, July 1.
4. All work will be inspected and approved by the county inspector before the final one-third payment will be made.
5. The bid proposal will serve as the contract for setting out the specifications of the job.

We're delighted to have you on the team. If you need anything our office can provide, just ask.

The most frequent use of the direct message strategy is to request information. In order for commerce to occur, information must be exchanged. Buyers need to know what suppliers have to sell; suppliers need to get information from manufacturers; shippers need shipping rates; advertisers need advertising rates; international bankers need exchange rates. Direct message strategy works the best for obtaining information.

A special case is requesting information about other people, as in pre-employment checks of references. In this case, legal and ethical considerations require the requester to include some additional content in the letter. To protect both the individual about whom the reference is written and the person writing the reference, the following must be included:

1. You must tell the person who is being asked to supply the reference whether the applicant has **authorized the request.** For example, "Cheryl Darice has given me your name as a person who could tell me about her preparation for a position as Charge Nurse in our Emergency Medicine Dept."

2. You must state clearly whether the information will be **kept confidential**. For example, "Of course, any information you provide will be kept confidential."

3. You must ask only questions directly **related to the position** the applicant will be performing. If you are looking for a salesperson, you

might ask "Does the applicant have the excellent interpersonal skills needed to succeed in a sales position?" If you were interviewing for a civil engineer who will spend most of the day working alone at a computer, a question about interpersonal skills might not be job related.

The law specifically forbids companies to make hiring decisions based on certain non-job-related factors such as race, religion, age, creed, sex, or handicap. You must not ask "Is the applicant, to the best of your knowledge, pregnant?" "Does the applicant belong to a union?" "Is the applicant a good Christian?" These are considered irrelevant to the applicant's ability to perform at a high level of competence.

Routine Claims and Adjustments

Because not everything runs perfectly in business, it will occasionally be necessary for you to write a claim letter, asking in a confident way that a situation be corrected. Since most claim letters are considered routine, the direct message strategy is the strategy of choice. For example, if you purchased a computer with a 90-day warranty, and on day 14 the screen locked up, you would write a direct message strategy claim letter. Although no one would argue that the message is good news for the receiver, it is routine. Some products will need to be repaired under warranty. On the other hand, if the warranty has expired and you want the company to repair your computer free anyway, that would *not* be routine, and an indirect persuasive message strategy would be called for.

Another example of a routine claim situation results when you order 24 glasses and two arrive broken. You have a routine and legitimate claim. Or perhaps you ordered 12 different items and wanted 6 each. What you got was a dozen each of 6 different items. This is another routine claim situation. The proper way to handle such a claim is to begin immediately with what you want. In the middle of your letter, state clearly all the facts as you understand them. Then close positively, restating your request. Here is an example of a routine claim letter that follows the direct message strategy:

Example 6.9

Please credit our account #45467 for $14.88.

On Monday, UPS delivered parcel 9990890, which contained 24 each of leaded glass wine goblets—Item #122321. Although the box looked in perfect order, the stems were broken on two of the glasses.

Normally we would prefer that broken merchandise be replaced. However, we ordered these glasses as part of a bridal promotion we're doing next week. Since the replacement glasses would not arrive in time for the promotion, we'd prefer your simply crediting our account.

Your fall catalog was included in the order. You have many exciting new products we look forward to ordering.

Notice that the tone of this letter is confident but not angry. The writer places no blame, makes no accusations, makes no unreasonable demands. Nor does the writer apologize or beg. This is a routine claim, best handled directly, assertively, and pleasantly. The writer begins with the assumption that since the claim is a fair one, the reader will respond positively.

If someone owes your company money which he has not paid within the usual time, the appropriate response is a direct routine claim letter. Assume the reader has overlooked the bill and will pay it as soon as you send the reminder. Make no threats and keep your tone positive. (If your direct message strategy claim letter does not produce the desired results, you will need to write a more persuasive indirect letter.)

Responding Positively to a Request

One final situation calls for a direct message strategy response—you are telling someone yes to a claim he or she has made. Suppose a customer has returned a suit to you, claiming something is wrong with the lining material. The customer has demanded a refund. You look the suit over and conclude the only problem with the lining is that a person too big for the suit coat has tried to put it on and stretched the lining beyond its ability to flex. The lining material has given way. You imagine that the purchaser has gained some weight or has loaned the coat to someone too big for it. Certainly you could say no to the claim. On the other hand, you would like to retain the customer's goodwill, so you decide to grant a refund. Once you have made the decision to say yes, say so with positive tone. Here is an example, first of how *not* to handle the situation, then of how to apply the direct message strategy.

Example 6.10A

I certainly agree that something is wrong with the lining of your suit coat. I disagree that our material is the problem. It looks to me as if you've put on some weight and the lining material just couldn't take the punishment you gave it.

Because we want to keep you as a customer, we're sending you a refund anyway. Please make sure you are fitted by an expert salesperson when you go suit shopping or you may find this problem occurs again.

Thank you for your patronage of our fine dress clothes products.

Example 6.10B

Enclosed is a refund for your suit. We're sorry you had an unfortunate experience with one of our products.

I have called Outfits Unlimited, the distributor of our suits in your area. If you will ask for Gordon Johnson, manager of Outfits Unlimited, when you are ready to purchase another suit, he will personally see that you receive the best quality and best fit for your suit dollar.

Outfits Unlimited is located at 26 S. Beach St. They are open from 10:00 a.m. to 6:30 p.m. Monday through Saturday. Please write if I can be of any further assistance.

Example of a
Goodwill Letter

226 W. 29th Avenue
Durham, NC 30045
September 16, 1993

Dear Thomas:

Congratulations on your promotion!

I remember how hard you worked on that computer analysis project. Having the organization recognize your dedication and the quality of your work must make you feel very proud.

I look forward to hearing all about your new responsibilities.

Sincerely,

Greg Gomez

Greg Gomez

Example of a
Response to an
Inquiry

Tomorrow's Computer Solutions
567 Eagle Blvd.
New Rochester, ID 88945
Call toll free (800) 524 - 8989

February 11, 1991

Dr. Michael Irvine
Suite 310
788 Rio Lindo Ave
New Rochester, ID 88946

Dear Dr. Irvine:

Here are the answers to the questions you posed about the Macintosh IIci. Thank you for your inquiry.

1. The IIci uses 68030 and 68882 microprocessors. This combination has received excellent reviews because of its speed, reliability, and color capability.

2. The standard IIci is equipped with 1 megabyte of RAM and a 1.4 megabyte floppy disk drive.

3. You can expand the IIci's memory to 8 megabytes RAM and increase its power for handling large tasks by adding a 40 or 80 megabyte internal hard disk.

4. You can choose from a variety of keyboards. The most popular is the Extended Keyboard which has 15 special function keys, cursor movement keys, and a built-in numeric keypad.

5. The IIci uses the Macintosh system software, making it instantly compatible with all other Macintosh versions. As a result, all the software and data documents which you have developed using your original Mac 512K will work on the IIci. In addition, you can order the A/UX operating system, Apple's implementation of AT&T UNIX, extending the Macintosh interface to that operating system.

The enclosed reviews of the IIci might interest you because they were published last month in two of the leading computer magazines. Harry Staple, our expert in medical office software, would be pleased to give you a demonstration of the IIci. Just give him a call at (766) 891-1630 to set up an appointment.

Yours truly,

Walter Lee

Walter Lee
Customer Service

*W*hen you expect the reader of your letter will be pleased with what you have to say, use a direct message strategy. Begin immediately. State your reason for writing in the first sentence.

Use the middle of your letter to provide additional information or to expand on your request. Arranging the middle part of a direct message letter into a list or a series of similarly phrased points will help your reader understand you.

Close with something positive about your future relationship with the reader. Use your ending to develop goodwill.

EXERCISES

1. You are planning to apply for a new job. As part of preparing for job hunting, you recognize the need to ask people to write recommendations for you. Applying the direct message strategy, write a letter to someone who might be willing to write a letter on your behalf. As part of your explanatory material, tell your reader the kind of position you plan to apply for. Also suggest qualities you hope your reader will be able to comment on. If you have not seen this person for some time, be sure to explain what you have been doing recently.

2. Write a goodwill letter of congratulations to someone you know.

3. You want to start a retail sporting goods store. You'll need suppliers. You know a great deal about a number of sports. You have business coursework. You have worked as a clerk in a sporting goods store. You do not, however, have much experience with suppliers and what they require to sell their products through your retail store. Write a letter of inquiry to the sporting goods manufacturer of your choice, finding out how you can go about carrying the company's products.

4. Write to a hotel to ask for reservations for an upcoming holiday. Be sure to include enough information so your reader can help you.

5. Valentine's Day is in ten days, and the restaurant you manage has advertised a Sweetheart Special—every woman will receive a fresh flower corsage, each meal will include free champagne, a popular local band will play romantic music, each couple will get a free picture, and the restaurant will be decorated with hearts and flowers. At least that was the plan. Two weeks ago you ordered the decorations from a major party-supplies company. Today, the order arrived. You eagerly opened the box to discover a complete set of Thanksgiving decorations. Everything is orange and brown. Instead of hearts and bows, you find turkeys and pumpkins. You must do something immediately. Calling the company seems the most expedient

thing to do. Outline your conversation, including the information you need and the claim you will make.

6. You work for a retail company that sells major and minor appliances—everything from stoves and washing machines to miniature tape recorders and electric razors. Your company has been in business for twenty-five years. The owner wants to have a big anniversary party and sale to thank the customers. Over the years, the store has developed a very good mailing list. You have been assigned the task of writing the letter which will invite the people on the mailing list to the party. Everything in the store will be for sale at 30 percent off. Seven door prizes will be given to people who attend. The grand prize is the winner's choice of a big-screen television with a video disc player or a side-by-side refrigerator-freezer with ice and water available through the door. Both choices are worth about $1,200. The party will be held Saturday, 6 p.m. to midnight. Food and drink will be served.

7

Negative Situations

In this chapter, you will learn about a message strategy to use when the receiver of your message will be disappointed. Based on the communication principle that first is a position of emphasis, you will not begin with the bad news. This strategy suggests an indirect beginning.

Once a sender has communicated disappointing news, he or she must be willing to expend extra effort to reestablish goodwill. As a result, the end of a negative news message is very important. In this chapter, you will learn how to use an indirect message strategy to deliver disappointing news without permanently damaging your goodwill.

INDIRECT MESSAGE STRATEGY

None of us likes to receive a *no* answer when we ask for something, whether for credit, a favor, an adjustment, or a job. Therefore, *saying* no and keeping the person as a friend or customer poses special problems. Fortunately, the number of situations where we must say no is relatively small. When, as a result of your pre-communication audience analysis, you believe your reader would prefer not to hear your message, the **Indirect Message Strategy** is the appropriate approach.

Indirect Strategy Situations

Some situations where you are most likely to use this strategy:

- refusing credit
- refusing a claim against the company

- telling someone he or she didn't get the job, promotion, raise
- saying you can't fill an order, repair a product, give time or money

In all these situations, the reader is likely to be disappointed to hear your news. When people are disappointed, they often get angry, blame the bearer of the bad news, defend themselves, and in other ways protect their egos. When they are busy defending, they are no longer listening to you and your message. They are too busy listening to the very loud voices inside.

The excellent communicator, therefore, takes care delivering bad news, presenting the message indirectly. Indirect presentation of negative news allows the receiver to get ready to hear it. It allows the receiver to save face.

In many cultures, the need to save face is so important it is an overt part of cultural training. The Japanese, for example, do not push one another into a position where they must say no. They determine negative news from the context in which a message is presented.

In the United States, we sometimes forget how important it is to help others save face. With careful presentation of bad news, we can help our reader save face and thus retain goodwill. This chapter discusses methods that will help accomplish these goals.

General Advice

Some general advice when using the indirect message strategy:

- Avoid negative phrasing and negative language.
- Avoid trite language.
- Don't use "company policy" as your reason for saying no.
- Pay special attention to your *tone*—work carefully not to offend or anger the reader.
- *Retain the reader's goodwill.*

People take a personal risk when they ask for something, whether that something is a job, a loan, a refund, or a date. When you must refuse their request, your goal is to indicate by your tone that your response is not personal. That is, your refusal is for reasons that have nothing to do with the requester's goodness, worthiness, or soul. One way to ensure a caring tone is to avoid trite, simplistic language. When your response is trite, the receiver of the message quite rightly believes you did not take the request as seriously as it was made. Avoid expressions like *surely you must agree that* or *as anyone can plainly see*, or *I'm surprised that you*. Such language puts the reader on the defensive.

Another general observation about bad-news messages is that they are usually longer than direct request messages. To pad or soften the bad news, you will need to spend longer with your reader. Think about a telephone call where you invite someone to dinner. You ask if your friend would like to come to dinner. Your friend says, "Let me check my calendar—yes, that would be great. When would you like me to be there?" You respond, "How about six?" Your friend says, "Good. Can I bring anything?" You say, "No thanks. Just yourself. See you Saturday." That's the end.

On the other hand, imagine how long the conversation will last when you call your family to say you will be unable to come home during this summer's vacation. First you'll want to prepare them for the news. Then, after you tell them, you'll need to stay on the phone to respond to their concerns, to reexplain, to reassure, to offer an alternative, and perhaps to assure them once again that your decision doesn't mean you don't care. That's the way it is with business letters that deliver negative news. You have to spend enough time with your reader to reestablish the relationship.

The Strategy

I. Use a buffer beginning.

Rather than beginning with the bad news, use your beginning to establish harmony with the reader. Talk about something neutral on which you and the reader can agree. The objective of the buffer beginning is twofold. First, you want to establish some common ground—some point of agreement. Second, you want to slow the pace of your writing down so the receiver has time to adjust to a possibly negative outcome. One of the principles of communication is that shorter sentences have more punch than long ones. In the delivery of negative news, you might try making your sentences a bit longer. That reduces the impact of any one word and slows the reader down.

In planning your beginning, you might be able to base the buffer on a statement the person made in the letter you received. For example, "You're right. It is annoying when no one returns your calls." You can make a statement of fact: "Nearly 80 people applied for the Secretary II position." You can even pay the reader a compliment as long as it doesn't cross the line from neutral to positive and lead the reader to believe positive news is coming. For example, "The work done by the United Way makes this community a better place for us all" is probably neutral enough that you can later say you cannot make a donation at this time. On the other hand, "I believe every citizen should contribute to the United Way's important work" is too positive to lead logically to a refusal to contribute.

The buffer must logically lead to your reasons for saying no. As a result, many writers find it easier to write the rest of the letter first, then go back and add a buffer beginning that flows into the next paragraph. If you have trouble beginning your negative-news messages, you might try writing the buffer last.

II. Tell the reader your reasons for saying no.

Before you say no, explain *why* you are refusing. In this section of your letter, your goal is to explain the reasons so clearly that the reader begins to accept the logic and sensibility of your answer. When the reader can see that you are not attacking or being unreasonable or ignoring his or her request, you are more likely to retain the reader's goodwill. If perfection in negative-news writing could be reached, your reasons would be so logical and your presentation of them so fair that by the time you actually said no, the reader would be thinking, "Of course, I knew that. No is the only sensible response. If I were in the same situation, that's what I'd say too."

Your explanation of your reasons can go awry in three ways.

DON'T APOLOGIZE

First, use a confident tone. Avoid apologizing. If you have good reasons for saying no, the reader will accept those more easily if you deliver them with confidence. All parents know about the whining child who responds to reasons with pleas like "It's not fair." Most parents also know their children are most likely to respond with whining when the parental explanation lacks conviction. When the parent "means business," the child knows right away and doesn't argue the point. So deliver your reasons clearly and without apology. (If you are unsure that refusing a request is the proper thing to do, then perhaps you should say yes. Before you begin a refusal letter, clarify the need to say no.) Your confidence will help your reader deal with the denial.

DON'T TELEGRAPH THE NO

To follow the indirect message strategy, the reasons **must** come before the no. If you preface your reasons with a word like *unfortunately* or phrases like *although we'd like to, your request is interesting, however*, or *in spite of our desire to*, you have told the reader that a no is coming. As a result, the reader is feeling very defensive before you ever get to your logical reasons. Avoid telegraphing the no before you have stated your reasons.

DON'T RELY ON COMPANY POLICY

Nothing makes people madder than "the system" and its "policies." We feel helpless and defenseless when the reason we can't have what we want is that some uncaring system says so without even knowing us or the facts of our case. If you want to retain goodwill, don't rely on company policy as your reason for denying someone something.

Of course, in real organizations most *nos* are the result of a company policy. If someone applies to your credit card company asking for an account, your decision will be based on company policy or standards of creditworthiness. Rather than telling your customer that, tell your customer the reasoning behind the policy. For example, rather than "based on company policy, we cannot approve your request," say "we have found that people who make over $20,000 per year are the best risks."

III. State the no.

Using positive language, subordinate clauses, passive voice, and so on, to develop a sensitive tone, say no or give the bad news. Although you are encouraged to reduce the emphasis on the negative news, don't bury the refusal in double-talk, excuses, or apologies. If your earlier explanation was accurate and logical, the reader will understand and accept your answer. You may imply the negative news without actually saying no only if you are certain that your response is clear. Nothing would be worse than to leave the reader unsure whether you said yes or no.

Remember the power of positive phrasing. Rather than talking about what you cannot do, talk about what you can do. Rather than "We cannot offer you the position," say "We have offered the position to a candidate with an M.B.A. and three years of supervisory experience." Rather than "We cannot approve your request for credit," say "As soon as you have been in business for two years, we will be happy to review your application for an open account. Until then, you will receive our 2% discount for cash purchases." Rather than "I'm sorry that I will be unable to speak to your club members," say "I have already committed to a speaking engagement in Chicago that day."

IV. Whenever possible, offer alternatives.

The sensitive communicator realizes that had he or she been able to say yes, the reader's problem would be solved. However, since you must say no, you are causing a problem for the reader. Can you think of some alternative solution for the reader? If so, reestablish goodwill by offering alternatives. Sometimes this part of a negative news letter is referred to as "Resale." Try to "sell" the reader on the idea that your relationship is still a good one, even though you said no to this one request. For example, if you are unable to speak to the Marketing Association because you are already engaged on the day of its meeting, you might suggest the name of another good speaker, or you might suggest another time when you would be available.

V. Close on a positive note.

Do not repeat the negative news at the end. Don't apologize or in any way go back to the negative news. Remember that beginnings and endings are positions of emphasis. You want the reader to remember the positive, not the negative. So stick with a goodwill, positive ending paragraph.

Avoiding the negative at the end is critical to your success with the indirect message strategy. The job of the ending is to assure the reader that your relationship will continue in spite of this issue. In many situations the ending can be off the subject. For example, suppose you encouraged your friend to apply for a position that was open at your company. If your friend doesn't get the job, you are going to have to talk about it. And when you're done talking about it, you will probably switch the topic and talk about something you plan to do together in the near future. That assures both of you that the relationship is more important than this one negative outcome. So it is with the close of any negative news letter—stress the relationship and retain the goodwill.

To write effective Indirect Strategy letters:

- Begin with a buffer.
- State your reasons.
- Positively state the bad news.
- Offer alternatives or resale.
- End on a positive note.

Examples of Indirect Message Strategy

Following is an example of a negative news letter that is poorly done. The writer does not appear to understand the impact of his tone on the reader. Although the name of the university has been removed, everything else about this letter is as it was received by the applicant.

Dear Ms. Olson:

Thank you for the opportunity to review your application for admission to the graduate program at ABC University. Unfortunately, we are unable to offer you an opening in the program for this coming fall semester. Our decision is based on an applicant's apparent ability to succeed with a high degree of success. That decision is made by considering the applicant's undergraduate training, grade transcripts, GMAT test scores, letters of reference and from other pertinent sources.

In some areas of study, the number of openings is limited and not all qualified applicants can be accepted. Thus, the availability of faculty and resources is an additional consideration.

I hope you will be able to find alternative approaches to achieving your goals.

Sincerely,

The Director of Admissions

Here is a much better negative news letter. This letter follows the indirect message strategy by starting with a neutral statement and creating harmony with the reader. Reasons are offered before the positively phrased no. Alternatives are offered to assist the reader in solving her problem. The letter ends with a slightly off-topic goodwill ending.

Dear Ms. Carpenter:

The International Students Organization provides a wonderful opportunity for university students (and faculty) to learn about other cultures from experts—our exchange students. I was very pleased to receive your invitation to act as faculty advisor to ISO.

This semester I have been appointed to serve on the California Higher Education Council, a group of educators and business representatives who advise the governor on education issues. The appointment requires that I fly to Sacramento for three days each month. Since I continue to carry my usual teaching and research responsibilities, my calendar is very full. Given the reality of my schedule this semester, I believe your organization would be better served by having someone else as its advisor.

Do you know Dr. Alan Brighton in the Dept. of Sociology? He is a very energetic, young professor who takes a real interest in the students. I think he might do an excellent job for you. His office hours are Tues/Wed/Fri 10:00–11:30, and his office extension is 4661. I took the liberty of telling him you might be giving him a call.

I am looking forward to seeing you and the other members of ISO at the spring Celebration of Nations. You always have such interesting speakers that week.

Sincerely,

Margaret Juarez

Margaret Juarez

The following is another good example of bad news delivered with grace and sensitivity:

To: Kevin Perkins, Manager, Milling Dept.

From: J. J. Eldridge, CEO

Subject: Four-Day Week Proposal

Date: October 22, 1993

Thanks very much for forwarding your proposal for a four-day work week for your department. I appreciate the creative energy—you always provide us with good ideas.

My data suggest that the 10-hour, four-day workweek would result in uneven customer service at a time when excellent customer service seems desirable. As you are aware, the recent increase in customer demand is presenting us with the right kind of problem: nearly constantly busy phone lines. My experience with other companies which have gone to the 10-hour day is that customers resent the lack of telephone assistance on Fridays, even though the longer day allows for easier connection with customers in the eastern time zones.

My concern for maintaining customer service makes me reluctant to implement your thoughtful suggestion now. However, I have asked our personnel department to review the data. Because of my respect for your leadership, I want to give all your ideas the most careful consideration.

Thanks again for taking the time to share your ideas with me. I appreciate your developing a very sound proposal at a time when I know you are quite busy.

Here's one final letter which applies the indirect message strategy in a desirable way.

Dear Retailer:

Thank you for ordering Gick's new Bead Shoppe collection of quality beads. Based on the orders we've been receiving from retailers like you, your customers appreciate the variety of colors and the quality of the beads.

These beads are manufactured in four different countries, one of which is Armenia. As you know, that country is suffering from internal strife. As a result, shipments of all blue-tone beads have been delayed. In order to keep your Bead Shoppe selection well stocked, we have arranged to have our Austrian manufacturer produce the blue-tone beads as well as the crystal and silver beads they now make. Shipments will begin arriving in the U. S. by air within ten days. You can expect your back-ordered beads within 15 working days.

As soon as the flow of beads is predictable and sufficient, we will once again offer beads in bulk to those retailers who prefer to package under their own brand. Enclosed is the spring catalog, just out, with a wide selection of wooden beads in both natural and bright, tropical colors—excellent for spring and summer beading projects. These beads are produced in Malaysia from nuts of the coco tree. You and your customers can feel confident that the rain forest is being protected. All spring catalog items are in stock and ready to ship.

*W*hen you have bad news to transmit, apply the Indirect Message Strategy. Begin your letter with a buffer, a neutral statement on which you and the reader can agree. This gets you started on the right foot.

Next, present the reasons you have for refusing a request or delivering bad news. Phrase your reasons confidently, without telegraphing the bad news. Avoid the "it's company policy" excuse.

Once you have carefully stated the reasons, positively phrase the actual rejection or refusal. Immediately move to possible alternatives and goodwill.

Remember that retaining the good relationship between you and your reader is your desired outcome. Use the ending position of emphasis to rebuild your goodwill with the reader.

EXERCISES

1. You have been invited to attend your cousin's wedding in early June. As it turns out, he has planned the wedding for exactly the day you are graduating. Write and explain that you will be unable to be at the wedding.

2. J. G. Westchester purchased a very expensive pair of ostrich-leather cowboy boots from your company. He has returned them, saying something is wrong with the leather on the toes. Upon inspection, you discover that he has dropped acid on the boots, perhaps from a damaged car battery. Although you guarantee your boots against defect in materials and work-manship, the damage on these boots is clearly not a problem with manufac-turing. Write to Mr. Westchester and deny his claim for a new pair of boots.

3. As a loan officer at a bank, you approve many loans. Almost all of them have a clause which says that if the borrower gets behind in the pay-ments, the bank has the right to declare the full amount of the loan due and payable. So far, you have never had to take this action. However, the branch manager, the loan committee, and you agree the action must be taken with the Lorilindas. They have made every payment late; they have missed the last two entirely; and now you hear they are planning to move to another state. Write a letter to the Lorilindas telling them the loan must be paid in full within thirty days or their car will be repossessed.

4. As a student, you have a special understanding of the concerns of students. That's why the dean of the college has asked for your help. Each year a number of students fall below the acceptable grade point and are put on probation. That means their grades must come up within one term or they will be dismissed from the university. The dean would like you to write the letter that will be sent to students whose grade point has fallen below the acceptable limit. Explain the consequences of being on academic probation (your catalog will give you the details).

5. Sam Walton (of Walmart) offers this success tip: underpromise and overdeliver. It's good advice which probably should have been followed. Instead, your boss seems to have promised one of Computer Solutions' major customers that you would go to his house next Saturday and help him install a memory board he recently bought. Your boss is out of town for the week, and he seems to have forgotten that you must be out of town next weekend—you're taking a training workshop in object-oriented pro-gramming. The only thing you can think to do is to write to Arthur Gee (the customer) and explain the situation. Of course, you'll leave a copy of the letter for your boss, so he'll know what you've done.

6. Assume you've been working for a company for 2 years. They seem to appreciate your work. You've received positive evaluations and two raises. However, now you've decided to get married and move with your new spouse to a town where you can both get good jobs. Write the letter in which you quit your job.

8

Writing to Persuade

In some situations, the receiver of your message might resist doing what you would like to have done. The reader might ask "Why should I?" When your audience analysis leads you to conclude that is the situation facing you, the persuasive message strategy is called for. This chapter discusses persuasive message strategy.

Persuasive message strategy takes an indirect approach. As with communicating negative news, you will need to overcome resistance to your message. Developing your message slowly and providing a great deal of reader benefit will help you overcome resistance.

PERSUASIVE MESSAGE STRATEGY

Many large organizations have advertising specialists who spend all their time writing sales and persuasive messages. However **all** managers and employees are called upon to write some persuasive messages. Persuasion is the act of gaining support or eliciting specific action from others.

Fifty years ago, managers could simply tell employees what to do ("boss" them around). However, modern managers understand that employees have options and must be *persuaded* to act. Certainly employees who want bosses to perform some specific action will need to persuade them. As a result, understanding the principles of selling is important to all business writers.

If, when you analyze your audience, you believe the audience will have a slightly defensive "why should I?" response to your request, the **Persuasive Message Strategy** is the appropriate strategy to use.

In all discussions of persuasion, the concept of manipulation is likely to arise. How ethical is persuasion? In what ways is it like or dissimilar to manipulation? In general, the difference is honesty. If your claims of reader benefit are legitimate, if you have not overstated or misstated the benefits the reader will receive from doing what you want nor understated any likely negative consequences, then you are getting what you want because others are getting what they want. You are setting up a win-win situation. Manipulation usually implies that someone is doing what you want without full knowledge of the personal consequences. Ethical business communicators seek win-win solutions to business problems.

Persuasive Strategy Situations

Some situations where you are most likely to use this strategy:

- selling a product or service
- selling an idea
- encouraging someone to give time, talent, or money to your project
- encouraging someone to vote for your candidate, idea, proposal
- job hunting—job application letters are sales letters

In each of these situations you are asking someone to do something because you want it. Your goal will be to convince the reader that he or she wants it as well.

We will specifically address the issues involved in writing a job application letter in Chapter 12, although the general principles discussed in this chapter apply in that persuasive situation.

General Advice

To persuade readers, you must sway them to your point of view. But if your readers believe that only you will benefit from the proposal, you will rarely be successful. You must demonstrate that the reader will benefit by acting. Some general advice to use with this strategy:

- Always use "you-attitude."
- Use examples, facts, quotations, pictures to demonstrate your point.
- Use color, underlining, boldface type, large type to catch attention..
- Stress the benefits to the reader.
- Use more imagery in your writing—help the reader "see," "taste," "hear," "smell," and "feel" the benefits.

Timothy Schellhardt, writing in the October 4, 1991, *Wall Street Journal*, says "Salespeople don't think letters get read, but that's because they don't write letters well." He cites the following as common mistakes: A weak opening, overuse of the word *I,* and failure to include benefits of a product or service. In this chapter, we'll discuss methods for overcoming those mistakes.

The Persuasive Strategy

I. Start with an Attention-Getting Beginning.

Everyone would like you to buy certain products, complete certain chores, vote for certain candidates, hire certain people. A lot of competition exists for the reader's time and attention. As a result, persuasive messages need to be very interesting right away. Grab the reader's attention with a powerful and interesting beginning. According to Allan A. Glatthorn, in *Writing for Success*, this is the "Hey You!" part of the letter.

ASK A QUESTION

Several approaches to attention-getting beginnings have proved themselves. Probably the most frequently suggested idea for a beginning is: Ask your reader a question that causes him or her to think. Here are some examples:

Example 8.1

How frequently does the average homeowner paint the exterior of the house?

In which month are the greatest number of people born?

If you could make environmental policy decisions, would you encourage or disallow offshore oil drilling?

Questions really catch the attention of U.S. citizens. For some reason, we find it hard not to try to answer them. Maybe it is a behavior learned from many years of school. Even the punctuation of a question, the question mark, is a hook, ready to catch readers and hold their attention.

If you use the question beginning, take care to ask a question that cannot be answered with a simple yes or no. For example, "Would your family like to try recycling?" might be answered with a rapid "No." The result is your letter goes in the trash and the rest of your great message goes unread. Instead think of a question which causes your reader to pause and think.

REFER TO FACTS

Relevant facts, examples, or assertions are good to include in your beginning. Humans seem to be internally driven to learn and grow. When you relay an interesting bit of information, most readers will be willing to see what comes next. Here are some examples of beginnings which refer to facts:

Example 8.2

Car and Driver, Road and Track, and *Automobile Week* all rate the new Chrysler in their Year's Top Ten Autos.

Fewer than 2 percent of the population controls nearly 30 percent of the financial resources.

Five-year, fixed-rate certificates of deposit earn less than 5 percent. At the same time you are making so little on your money, the bank is charging 14.3 percent on secured three-year automobile loans.

These statements of interesting fact do the same thing asking a question does; they get the reader involved and willing to expend the effort to read your message.

EXPERT OPINION

When you are trying to persuade someone to do what you want, the reader may wonder about your credibility. One way to overcome resistance to your ideas and to catch the reader's attention is to begin by relying on a known expert's opinion. For example, many over-the-counter medicines are advertised by saying "More hospitals provide this product to their patients than any other brand." The hospital staff is considered to be expert in matters of medicine. Racecar drivers are used to advertise motor oil. Sports figures are used to advertise sporting equipment.

In business letters, you might refer to known experts in the field of business. Quotations from Lee Iacoca, Peter Drucker, Tom Peters, and Sam Walton are frequently used to start letters. You might even begin collecting interesting quotations, noting who made the comment and where, so you have a resource base to draw from in the future. Here are some examples and an idea for using them:

Example 8.3

In a letter from management to union to encourage another round of talks:

"That old law about 'an eye for an eye' leaves everybody blind."

Martin Luther King, Jr.

To begin a letter to Democrats about getting the local party organized for upcoming elections:

"I am not a member of any organized political party. I am a Democrat."

Will Rogers

For a letter encouraging investors to buy shares of a money fund:

"If you can actually count your money then you are not really a rich man."

J. Paul Getty

VARIATIONS IN TYPE

You might also want to use different typefaces, a touch of color, or underlining to catch the reader's attention. Every professionally prepared sales letter relies on these techniques. You can too. Sometimes a very small bit of color, added after your message is typed, can really catch attention. For example, you might try underlining just one or two words in your first paragraph with a red or blue marker. Good words to emphasize are *you* and words which refer to the need you believe your product or idea can meet, such as *save* or *reward*.

Research on readability indicates two important cautions to using variations in type: (1) All capital letters are hard to read. Avoid using this method of emphasis because it will work against you. When we read, we are seeing patterns or shapes. The letters that reach above the midline—like *d, t, h, b,* and *l*—and the letters that reach below the midline—like *g, y, p,* and *q*—help give different shape to different words. When you CAPITALIZE EVERY WORD, THE SHAPE IS LOST, AND READING IS MADE MORE DIFFICULT. The general rule: Never capitalize more than three words in a row. Perhaps it is better not to use this technique at all. (2) Avoid the use of italics. Except when you specifically want your typing to appear more like handwriting, *words written in italics appear lighter and finer* and are thus harder to read. When readers are taxed, they often just jump over the very words you were hoping to emphasize. Instead, use underlining or **boldface type**. In research, color tests as the most emphatic, and boldface type is second best.

II. Identify potential reader need.

It will be more difficult to demonstrate the benefits of your idea or product if you haven't told the reader what need or needs you can fill. Some of the most compelling needs:

to be loved
to be powerful
to be one of the group

      security
      money
      prestige and status
      to feel competent
      to feel free of stress

In the first paragraph or two of your message, remind the reader of a need you believe your product or idea can fill. Here are some examples:

Example 8.4

BMW sells its cars by filling the need for status. It sells "The Ultimate Driving Machine."

Volvo sells its cars by filling the need for security. It sells the car ranked safest by Consumer's Union.

General Motors sells the Geo Metro by filling the need to save money. It sells the car which gets the best gas mileage of any car in the United States.

Using Glatthorn's language, this is the "you've got an itch" part of the letter. You remind the reader of a need.

III. Demonstrate the benefits.

Using as much imagery (picture words) as possible, provide sound evidence to prove that the reader (or company) will benefit by accepting your proposal. Show how your product or idea will fill the need you've identified. This section of your letter may be several paragraphs long. It might take many benefits to overcome the reader's resistance. Each time you discuss a quality or characteristic of your proposal, indicate how the reader benefits from that quality or characteristic. This process is called psychological interpretation. Except for the first sentence of your letter, the ability to show the reader how the qualities apply directly to his or her situation is the most important part of your message. Here are some examples of psychological interpretation. To make the difference between the quality of the product and its benefit clear to you, the benefit has been printed in boldface type.

Example 8.5

This refrigerator comes with the easy-clean surface—**no more sticky fingerprints on the door.** You can also change the upper and lower front panels so **your refrigerator will match your decor even if you change the color of the kitchen.**

This sturdy luggage weighs only 3.2 pounds—**you'll be hopping on and off Europe's trains with ease**. And if you find a special bargain, the expandable feature of the Pullman **will make it easy for you to bring your bargain home. No need to arrange shipping in a foreign country.**

The winter ocean is spectacular after a storm. And because winter is off-season, **you can save more than half the cost of a similar summer trip to the sea**.

If you think the reader might have some objections to your idea or product, make sure you provide counterarguments or evidence. You might, for example, say "The grapevine seems convinced that layoffs are unavoidable. I've got the figures to prove we can keep everyone employed and still remain profitable."

Discuss price in the middle section of your letter, indicating the value of the product at the same time. Most people consider cost the most negative part of any proposal. Putting your discussion of cost in the middle reduces the emphasis it gets and allows you time to reiterate the benefits afterward. The experts suggest making the price appear as low as possible. According to the December 28, 1992, issue of *Fortune*, even consumers of high-priced items do cost comparisons and choose the product with comparable quality and lowest price.

One way to make the price seem lower is to say "Three easy payments of only $17.98—and that includes shipping and handling" rather than "A very reasonable price of only $ 53.94." Others recommend separating shipping and handling: "And the price for all this incredible music is only $9.95, plus $3.95 for shipping and handling." How you handle the costs of a proposal, whether they are in money or time, may determine whether you are seen as ethical and credible or unethical and manipulative. Obviously you want your proposal to appear in the best light. On the other hand, avoid trickery.

In Glatthorn's words, this is the "which I can scratch" part of the letter. Tell your reader, in your most psychologically relevant way, how your proposal will meet his or her needs.

IV. Call for action.

Since you wrote a persuasive message to encourage the reader to take a particular action, make certain you tell the reader specifically what you want him or her to do. Make your tone confident and direct. And then quit. Once you have stated clearly what you want, stop. Resist the temptation to add things like "Thank you for your consideration" or "We look forward to your business." Here are some examples of call-for-action endings:

Example 8.6

Call now. Operators are standing by.

All you need to do is sign the enclosed card and drop it in the mail.

If you want to take advantage of this special stock offering, call your broker or send the enclosed authorization certificate directly to Custom Corp.

On November 4, cast your vote in favor of education. Vote for Candice Brownelle.

You might want to use your last paragraph to accomplish several things in addition to calling for action.

END DATING

People seem to procrastinate. Writers of persuasive messages have found that even when they have done an excellent job of convincing, some readers will just never get around to taking the required action. One approach that helps is to give the reader a time frame—a date by which the action must be taken. Some typical examples: "Sale ends June 30." "Let's get together and talk about this before Friday's big meeting." "The issue date is April 1. Investors who wish to use this fund as part of their tax-sheltered annuity plan must sign a contract of investment before April 15."

REFER BACK TO THE BEGINNING

A persuasive message looks well thought out if in the last paragraph you go back to the need you identified in your beginning. A well constructed persuasive message improves your credibility with the reader. Here are some examples: "So if you need a break from the stresses of your hectic life, come visit us in sunny, relaxed St. Croix." "If you agree with me that it's time for management and labor to get together on this issue, tell your shop steward you want the union back at the table." "If, like 23 percent of the population, you were born in July, this is the most important self-study book you can buy."

MAKE TAKING ACTION EASY

Make it easy for the reader to take action. For example, include a reply envelope, offer to drive the reader to the polling booth, or offer a toll-free telephone number. Research shows that many order blanks have been filled out and envelopes addressed for orders that never made it to the retailer. The customer didn't have a stamp at the time and never quite got around to mailing the order. Preaddressed postage-paid envelopes make taking action easy. The receiver of a persuasive message believes the writer ought to be willing to do some of the work to get what he or she wants. If you want a colleague at work to read over a report you've written before you give it to the boss, take the report to your colleague, then go pick it up. If you want a customer to order by phone, provide a toll-free number and perhaps have someone available to answer the phone before and after normal business hours. Make taking action easy.

Above all, make your call for action clear and specific. In Glatthorn's language, this is the "if you come over here" part of the letter.

To write effective Persuasive Strategy letters,

- Begin with an attention-getter.
- Identify reader need.
- Demonstrate benefits which fill reader need.
- Call for action.

HARD OR SOFT SELL

Discussions of persuasive message strategy sometimes divide the subject into **persuasion** and **sales**. Others might call these soft sell versus hard sell. In either case, the general strategy is the same. What differs is tone and word choice. The hard-sell sales letter moves faster, is more direct in its language, has a tone of "Let's do it right now." The sentences in a hard-sell letter will be shorter. In fact, many "sentences" in sales letters are not sentences at all. They are phrases. The reader is hurried along, encouraged to make a decision right away and take the required action.

Soft sell or persuasion must accomplish the same goals of overcoming resistance and encouraging action. The process just moves more slowly. The tone of a soft-sell letter will be friendlier, more personable, perhaps more collaborative. The call for action might be "Let's get together and see if we can reach a win-win situation." Soft sell is much more effective when you want to project an image of being sensitive to others' needs.

Examples of Persuasive Message Strategy

Example 8.7 Hard-Sell Sales

The Atherton Corporation
27 Park Plaza Court
Sweet Home, OR 98888
March 14, 1993

Mr. Kyle S. Coberg
Uptown Upholstery
334 W. Huston Avenue
Detroit, Michigan

Dear Mr. Coberg:

A 61% return on sales—that's what retailers who carry Atherton's line of quality upholstery fabrics make. Many manufacturers are raising their prices on textiles. And many retailers will lose customers if they pass those price increases on. The result? The retailer makes less and less.

You can stop the erosion of your profits. In fact, you can dramatically increase them. Atherton manufactures excellent quality upholstery fabrics, and we do that right here in the United States. You can expect the superior feel, wear qualities, and color-fast dyes the U.S. textile industry is famous for. And you can get it for less.

Over the last three years, Atherton has installed completely computerized weaving equipment. The result is significantly lower costs and the highest quality possible. Because we don't need to ship our fabric from overseas and pay import duties, you get the best for less.

Enclosed is our catalog of over 350 fabrics, all suitable for in-house or direct retail use. Look at the wide variety of material types in the latest designs and the richest colors. Our terms are 2/10, net 45. We ship by U.P.S. unless you request an alternative. Over 90% of our orders are shipped next day, so you can get right to work on special-order projects. If you're ready to increase your return on sales dramatically, call toll free (800) 434-6100 to place your order.

Sincerely,

Katherine Blalock

Katherine Blalock
Marketing Vice President

Example 8.8 Soft-Sell Persuasion

To: Ted Gee

Plant Operations

From: Jesus Martinez

Janitorial

Date: October 23, 1993

Subject: Budget Preparations

Why is there never enough money in a budget? I've been going over the list of improvements my team would like to have funded in the new budget. You won't be surprised to hear we won't have enough money to get to the entire list. And that's the problem I could use your help with.

Last year when we were preparing for the budget, you mentioned that each year you hold back ten percent of the monies to cover any emergencies which might arise. The better my group keeps things repaired, the fewer emergencies we're likely to face. That reduces your headaches and those desperate calls in the middle of the night. What would you think about transferring any emergency-fund money which was left from this year into next year's improvement budget? The benefits would be both short term and long term.

In the short term, you would see immediate results. For example, the ceiling in your office could be repaired. Since it isn't one of those situations which will get worse if it's left unattended, we wouldn't deal with it if money is short. Of course, the reality is it's an eye-sore—just the kind of thing which might turn off a potential customer who stops by to talk with you about our ability to meet a production deadline. And that's a long-term cost which a larger repair and improvement budget can eliminate.

I'd really appreciate talking to you about this idea before we have to go into those budget hearings next week. Can we meet Thursday at 2:00? I'll call Linda and have her put me on your schedule.

More and more situations call for a persuasive approach. Buyers and sellers, managers and laborers, engineers and marketers must all work toward win-win solutions. The persuasive message strategy provides a technique for reaching win-win outcomes.

When your audience might respond with resistance to your idea or *request, use the persuasive message strategy. Begin with an interesting attention-getting opening. Remind your reader of the need your product, idea, or service might fill. Then provide evidence which demonstrates how the product, idea, or service meets the need.*

When you have provided enough reader benefit to convince the reader, close with a call for action. Make it as easy as possible for your reader to take the action you desire.

EXERCISES

1. Write to your congressional representative and encourage him or her to vote for a bill you support.

2. You took your car to Bee Gee's Auto Repair to have the timing adjusted three weeks ago. The charge: $49.95. You picked up your car, drove it home, and listened nervously to a definite "ticking." The next morning, you returned your car and explained the noise. Bee Gee said he'd check it out. When you returned to get your car, you had another bill, this time for $63.00. It seems you needed a new fan belt. This afternoon, while washing your car, you noticed a screwdriver resting on a motor mount. The chances are excellent that the ticking was caused by an errant screwdriver as it worked its way past the fan to land on the motor mount, rather than by a worn fan belt. Write to Bee Gee and see if you can persuade him to return the portion of the $63.00 that was for labor. Since you indeed have a new fan belt, you believe it is fair that you pay for the part ($22.25).

3. Write a letter to the editor of your school newspaper encouraging your fellow students to vote in an election.

4. Write a sales letter which you can put under the windshield of Japanese cars that encourages the car owners to try your Rising Sun Auto Repair. You specialize in repairing Japanese cars and small trucks. You keep a large inventory of parts on hand.

5. Write a letter that encourages others to join any organization of which you are a member.

6. In your garage workshop, you have developed an entirely new method for cutting fabric, leather, even wire. It wouldn't be accurate to refer to your product as scissors, because the tool is actually a tiny laser. You have made 25 of your new cutters. If you could make these in batches of 100, you could get the price down to $49.95 each. That's a lot of money for scissors. However your cutters can easily be used by people with restricted hand movement or with very weak hand muscles, such as people with arthritis. Determine your best audience; then write a sales letter directed to them.

9

Writing for Special Situations

Two additional writing situations are faced by most managers: preparing press releases and writing instructions. Both situations use a variation on the direct message strategy. However, although they begin immediately, both press releases and instructions require writers to apply some special strategies.

In this chapter, you will learn the additional strategies that will make your instructions clear and easy to follow and your press releases more likely to end up in the newspaper, on TV, or on the radio.

WRITING INSTRUCTIONS AND PROCEDURES

Managers direct the work of others. Much communication with their subordinates and some communication with their colleagues centers around telling them what to do and how to do it. Some managers are better at instructing than others. Typically, the better instructors follow the suggestions made in this section.

Some situations where you are most likely to use this strategy:

- explaining how to do one aspect of your job
- explaining to a new employee how to perform his or her job
- explaining to employees how to use their employee benefits
- explaining safety procedures
- explaining new procedures

General Advice

Some general advice to use with this type of strategy:

- Take nothing for granted.
- Do the process yourself or ask an expert to demonstrate it to you.

To be effective, instructions must begin at the beginning. It is better to provide a review for people who already know some of the information and risk boring them than it is to leave out some introductory material for someone who does not know. Apple Computer provides excellent training manuals for the purchasers of its computers. The manuals are organized with an introduction suggesting that purchasers who have experience with Apple Computer products can skip immediately to part 3. Parts 1 and 2 explain the general ways in which Apple computers work, including the mouse and the menu—information that remains constant from one Apple product to another. By arranging its manuals this way, Apple can begin at the beginning for brand new users of their products without slowing the learning of users who are familiar with the general concept and need to know just about one application.

Specific Advice for Instruction Writers

The effectiveness of all instructions and procedures will be improved if you apply the following ideas.

BE BRIEF

Say what needs to be done in as few words as possible. The more words you use, the more likely you are to include something that confuses. "Plug in toaster. Do not let cord rest on hot toaster" is much better than "Using the cord provided, and taking care not to let the cord come in contact with the toaster or any source of water, plug your toaster into a 110-volt electrical outlet." As long as you are selling your toaster in the United States, all the electrical outlets with a two-prong plug will be 110-volt. If purchasers don't know that, they may be concerned and wonder if they have the right voltage. In other words, don't say what doesn't need to be said. Keep your instructions brief.

AVOID JARGON

Jargon is language specific to a particular group or profession. When you are writing instructions, avoid jargon. Those needing the most instruction are those least likely to understand the jargon. When I was a new professor, I asked a librarian how to get copies of an article made. She said I needed a "calf form." Never having heard of such a thing, I didn't know if I already had one or needed to get one. If I needed to get one, I didn't know where to go. Learners are embarrassed to show their ignorance so will frequently not ask for clarification. (Later I found out a "calf form" was a charge authorization form—C.A.F.—available from my department secretary.)

BE SPECIFIC

In addition to saying what you want done briefly and in simple words, make your directions specific. If you want a proposal submitted by noon on Friday, say "The proposal must be on my desk by noon, Friday, October 12." Many supervisors are disappointed and many employees frustrated when the directions are "Try to get that to me Friday morning." What did the boss mean by "try"? What did the boss mean by "morning"? In fact, what did the boss mean by "to me," since she is regularly at headquarters downtown on Friday mornings? Is the proposal supposed to be delivered to her there?

Obviously all these issues are addressed when the instructions are specific. The easiest way to make your instructions brief, clear, and specific is to be well prepared before you begin writing. Think through the steps. Know what materials will be necessary. Know how long the process is likely to take.

USE COMPARISON AND ANALOGY

People learn much faster if the unknown process can be tied to a known process. Ask yourself how the new process is like something the learner already knows. Provide comparisons and analogies. For example, nearly all U.S. children learn to ride a bicycle. How is learning this new thing like learning to ride a bicycle?

Example 9.1

When you first learned to ride a bicycle, the more you thought about what to do to turn left, the shakier and more awkward your turn was. The best turns were when you just relaxed and turned left without thinking about how. Learning to type fast is much like turning left on the bicycle. Don't think about where the keys are and what you have to do to type faster. Just relax and let your fingers remember where the letters are. Concentrate on the words you wish to type.

Example 9.2

The chances are excellent that you fell several times while learning to ride a bicycle. Learning this skill is somewhat like learning to ride a bicycle. You should expect to "fall" several times. Be patient with yourself. Keep trying.

SUMMARIZE AND REPEAT

One of the issues in quality control is checking quality frequently so the amount of reworking necessary is small. When you give someone directions, it is helpful to summarize every few steps and clarify what a properly finished product would look like at this stage. "Once you have attached the brace at the top and bottom and tightened the bolts with the torque wrench, your assembly should look like a bookshelf with two cubes sitting on it."

The longer your set of instructions, the more important repetition and summary are. When the learner gets confused, he or she can go back to the last summary point where everything was OK and review what was done since then.

NUMBER THE STEPS

Present your instructions sequentially in the order in which they are to be done. Number the steps. This adds clarity and allows the learner to check off each step as it is completed. If you have more than about seven steps in your process, divide the steps into groups and use headings. Provide a summary at the end of each section.

USE DIAGRAMS, PICTURES, AND EXAMPLES

Providing visual cues is especially helpful. Diagrams, drawings, and photographs show the learner what the goal is. They are excellent for providing information about the three-dimensional nature of an assembly or a process.

Athletes train using videotapes, first of experts, then of themselves. The newest technology takes videotape of the athlete and computer enhances it so the athlete sees himself or herself doing the movement just right. That convinces the brain that perfection is possible and makes mimicking the movements remarkably easy. This training technology is very expensive. The concept, however, is the same when your instructions include pictures and diagrams of the goal.

Examples are a similar type of aid to learning and are used when the instructions involve learning *concepts* rather than *processes*. Textbooks use the method of providing examples to clarify instructions. You will find examples throughout this book. The example is most helpful if it relates to the learners and their situation or background. For example, a text that teaches medical students about how the immune system operates will probably include examples quite different from those in an auto mechanics book on how the internal combustion engine works. As with all other communicating tasks, start with audience analysis. Make your diagrams, pictures, and examples relevant to your audience.

Instruction-Writing Strategy

I. Provide an overview.

Begin each set of instructions with an overview, an introduction. Tell in a general way what the goal is: "Once you've learned the specific steps involved in writing clear instructions, you will find the job much easier, and your employees will be able to complete their tasks faster and with higher quality. Writing clear instructions involves knowing both your audience and the task you want the audience to complete." Here's another example from a cookbook, *The Complete Vegetarian Cookbook* (Pocket Books, 1974):

Example 9.3

Pancakes provide you with the opportunity to experiment with different grains, nuts and seeds. This often results in amazing and delicious tastes and textures. Top pancakes with fresh fruit, yogurt, honey butter, fruit butter, grated fruit, or preserves.

Pancakes should be cooked on a moderately hot griddle, lightly greased if necessary. Cook pancake until it has many bubbles on top and is lightly-browned on the bottom. Then turn it over and brown the other side.

Hint: Don't mix the batter *too* much. It should be slightly lumpy. Only turn pancakes one time on griddle.

II. List equipment needed.

You are certain to frustrate your learners if you let them get halfway through a project and then tell them they need a special tool available only at authorized dealers. List all the equipment needed, both supplies and tools, at the beginning of your instructions. This will help your reader get prepared and will also provide an idea of how complex the project is. Here is the list of ingredients from the pancake recipe in Example 9.3.

Example 9.4

2 cups milk
2 eggs, beaten
2 tablespoons oil
1 tablespoon molasses
2 tablespoons honey
1 1/2 teaspoons baking powder
1/2 teaspoon salt
1 1/2 cups buckwheat flour

III. List the steps in the process sequentially.

If your instructions are long and complex, number the individual steps. If the process is relatively short, you can use a narrative format. You will notice that textbooks use the narrative format of providing instructions and then group sets of instructions under different headings. Frequently each group of instructions begins with a short overview or introduction and ends with a summary or checkpoints. Here are the steps given in the recipe for pancakes:

Example 9.5

> In a large mixing bowl, mix all the liquid ingredients. Stir in baking powder, salt and buckwheat flour. If batter is too runny, add a little more flour. Cook on hot griddle.
>
> Yield: 10–12 cakes

In this example, you can see that audience analysis has led the author to make certain assumptions about the person following the instructions. The author assumes the reader will know what "liquid ingredients" are and what "too runny" is. In a cookbook for beginners, these terms might be explained. For example, the author might say "When you pour the batter onto the griddle, the batter should be about 1/4-inch thick. If the batter makes a cake thinner than that, you will need to add 1–2 tablespoons more flour."

IV. Provide summaries and checkpoints.

As mentioned before, summaries and checkpoints included within and at the end of your instructions allow the reader to check quality and correctness, thus reducing the reworking that would need to be done. When a particular step cannot be reworked if it isn't done right the first time, be sure to tell your reader so. Warnings are helpful.

On the other hand, don't overdo them, or the reader will soon overlook them. For example, highways are marked with "curve ahead" signs that provide information on how fast the driver should be going when he or she enters the curve. Most drivers soon learn that on clear days, they can safely exceed that speed by ten miles per hour. The danger with understating the safe speed is that drivers begin to make assumptions which get them in trouble when the curve really does demand the stated speed.

In summary, to write effective instructions,

- Analyze your audience.
- Know and understand the process you are teaching.
- Provide an overview.
- List the supplies needed.
- List the steps in order.
- Provide checkpoints and summaries.

PREPARING PRESS RELEASES

When a business has news it wishes to appear in the press or on television, it is customary for the business to initiate the article. Someone in the firm prepares a press release. A press release is a special form of writing because the writer must write in the style of the intended outlet. Newspapers present information in slightly different style from that of radio news. TV news almost always contains some videotape. The more like the style of the intended outlet you can make your press release, the greater your chance of having your article published as you have written it.

Many managers work to develop a good relationship with a newsperson at a local newspaper or television station. They know if they call that person when they have newsworthy material, that person is more likely to be supportive of the company when the company wants to have good news published.

Some situations where you are most likely to prepare a news release:

- introduction of a new product
- hiring a new manager
- a change in corporate strategy
- mergers and acquisitions
- selection of new directors
- release of new stock

Press Release Strategy

Press releases follow a particular format different from the usual letter format. This format includes the following information:

1. A heading that states in capital letters: NEWS RELEASE.
2. A statement of when the news can be released. Usually this line says "For Immediate Release" and is underlined.
3. The name and phone number of a contact person in the company.
4. The announcement in the style of the intended outlet. For a newspaper, the announcement includes a headline typed in capital letters.

The announcement should begin with a dateline—the city from which the story originated, followed by the date.

Press Release Style

A press release is typed on plain (not letterhead) stationery. Double-space to newspapers. Triple-space for radio and television audiences. A news story follows a strategy called the inverted pyramid style. The most important information is given first, with greater and greater detail provided as the story continues. Write in the third person—the writer does not appear in the story. For example, instead of "I interviewed the president of the company and he reported," say, "The president of the company reported."

News articles always cite the source for the information. When you write a news release, you must also cite sources. Providing direct quotations makes the story more interesting and supports the quality of the information. As the author of a press release, you will need to interview key people and ask permission to quote them. For example, suppose your winery is releasing a new varietal wine. You would like to see a story about this in the weekend food guide, so you prepare a press release. You would include information like the following:

Example 9.6

> RUTHERFORD HILLS, September, 1993—Vintners at Ed's Winery in Rutherford Hills announced today the release of a new chardonnay. Ed Chadswick, general partner, said to a group of wine merchants assembled at the winery, "We're really proud of this new varietal. It has character and bouquet equal to the best California can offer."

As your story develops, be sure to answer *who, what, where, when, why,* and *how.* Some newswriters claim that *why* and *how* are the least important ingredients to a good story.

If you are preparing a news release for television, a good-quality videotape of the president making some comments about the new product and perhaps a shot of the label would increase the likelihood of your story making the air.

In summary, to write effective press releases,

- Write in the style of the intended outlet.
- Write in the third person.
- Use quotations.
- Answer the questions *who, what, where, when, why,* and *how.*
- Start with the overall picture; then include increasing detail.

*B*usiness communicators may be called upon to write instructions and press releases. Each of these special situations calls for special strategies.

To write effective instructions, begin by providing an overview. List the equipment and supplies needed. List each of the steps in the process sequentially and provide regular summaries and checkpoints.

To prepare an effective press release, write in the style of the intended outlet. If you want your story to appear in a newspaper, include a headline. If you want your story to appear on television, include a video clip—a sound bite.

EXERCISES

Writing Instructions

1. More and more clocks use the digital format, but children still need to learn to tell time on analog clocks (if for no other reason, so they'll know which way clockwise is). Write a set of instructions for figuring out what time it is on an analog clock.

2. Write a set of instructions for the proper way to address an envelope. You can assume your audience is new employees in the typing pool.

3. Write a set of instructions which the bank you work for can include with customer statements, teaching customers how to balance their check-books.

Writing Press Releases

1. Assume the company you work for has an employee newsletter that is enclosed with each employee's biweekly paycheck. You would like to have an article included in the newsletter about how well the employees in your department are doing. They have improved their delivery time from four days to one and one-half days, and they have reduced the number of accidents in the department by 40 percent.

2. Carolyn Hatfield, the woman who has been CEO of your company for the last six years, is retiring and stepping down effective the first of next month. The company is pleased to announce that the current vice president of finance, Heath Stanton, has been chosen to take over the CEO position. Write a press release announcing these changes.

3. Your company has just donated $300,000 to the local university to assist in the purchase of chemistry equipment. You presented the check to the dean of the College of Chemistry at a luncheon today. Write a press release that announces this good-news event.

10

Employment Communication: Getting Ready

A special group of communication topics centers around the process of applying and being hired for a job. Communication about employment introduces several additional challenges for business communicators.

When you are seeking employment, there are no more important documents than your résumé and job application letter. That, combined with the overall tension associated with job hunting, make effective communication more challenging. We rarely do our best communication when we are tense.

Additionally, people seeking jobs must walk a very fine tightrope between a confident and a diffident tone. They must sound confident; at the same time, their tone must reflect an awareness that they are in the lower-status position.

In this chapter, you will learn some techniques for clarifying your job-hunting goals. In the following four chapters, we will address the different communication situations facing job seekers—the résumé, the job application letter, the interview, and the follow-up.

SETTING GOALS

Study after study indicates that those people who have written goals are more likely to feel satisfied with their lives. A ten-year study published in

1992 demonstrated that Harvard graduates who left school with written goals had significantly more financial wealth *and* feelings of satisfaction and happiness than those who did not clarify their goals.

Certainly in job hunting the evidence is conclusive: those who apply for a specific position and have a reasonable idea of the skills required for that position have a much greater chance of being employed than those who apply for work in general. Some job hunters believe that if they are open to whatever jobs a company has available, they will increase their likelihood of being employed. Evidence does not support this theory.

Clarifying Your Goals

The first step in effective job hunting is to decide what job you want. For many, both those who have never held a career position and those who have worked for years, clarifying what you want to do is very difficult. It is, however, very important. You will be spending one-third or more of your life at work. If you love your work, the rest of your life will be improved. If you dislike your work, the chances are excellent that the rest of your life will be negatively affected.

Many people in career counseling suggest that you take job hunting as seriously as you would take your job. Do your research; keep your information well organized. Begin by working on clarifying your job goals.

Career counselors suggest the following exercises to help you decide what your goal is. If you are currently unclear about what job you want to apply for, do these exercises.

Exercise 10.1

1. Write your obituary. Assume you have lived to the age of 110. What do you hope people will remember you for? What will they say about you in the newspaper?

2. Choose ten words to complete the following sentence: During his/her lifetime, __(your name)__ valued, prized, and held important _____ .

When you are done, rank-order your words, putting the most important first and the least important last.

3. Which of the following pairs more suits your working style?

standing/moving	sitting
indoors	outside
with people	alone
managing people	managing things/ideas
creativity/flexibility	predictability
quiet	busy
factory setting	office setting

having power/responsibility   being responsible for own work
high pressure   low pressure
following procedures   decision making

4. What are the skills you currently have which you believe would benefit an employer?

5. What were your three favorite courses in school? Why?

6. What do you like doing best in your leisure time? Why?

Books like *What Color Is Your Parachute?* by Bolles, and *Go Hire Yourself an Employer,* by Irish, offer many more ideas for clarifying what you want from a job. Write your answers in a notebook.

Researching Jobs

Once you have a definite sense of who you are, what you value, what you like, and your skills, the second step in clarifying your goals is to discover which jobs provide opportunities for doing what you love.

LIBRARY RESEARCH

Your library has a government publication, the *Job Titles Index*, that lists all the official job titles and offers a brief description of the task requirements of each. The library is also likely to carry "trade journals," magazines focused on specific industries. For example, if you think you would like to be in banking but are unclear of what specific job would interest you, you could read through several issues of *Banking, Savings and Loan*, or *The Financial Advisor*. These magazines will give you a sense of the kinds of jobs people hold in the banking industry. Every industry has its journals. The sewing and craft business, for example, has *Sew News* and *Profitable Craft Merchandising*. In addition to teaching you about the kinds of jobs available in an industry, trade magazines offer information on the career paths people typically take and on the job-specific jargon they use.

LETTERS OF INQUIRY

Another good idea for finding out what people with certain jobs actually do is to ask them. Many have been able to clarify what specific jobholders do by writing letters of inquiry.

Using the direct message strategy, write to someone who does a job you think you would like. Ask that person to tell you about the job, the preparation required, the strengths of the job and its weaknesses. Most people are glad to help. They are pleased you think the job they do is a job worth doing. Here's an example of a letter asking for information about a job:

Example 10.1

Dear Mr. Prince:

Would you please tell me a little about the work you do as an agent in the CIA? Based on library research, your job sounds interesting. It seems you make an important contribution to the country.

I am about to graduate with a degree in sociology. I served four years in the Air Force right after high school. I have frequently wondered if a position in the CIA would be the right one for me. I would really appreciate any help you can give me.

1. What kind of background—education and experience—is required to become an agent?

2. How long have you held this job?

3. What would you say are the three best things about your work?

4. What are the three things you like least about your job?

If you prefer talking on the phone, I can be reached almost every afternoon between 2:00 and 4:30 at (203) 665-9009.

Thank you so much. I really appreciate your time and help. Your efforts will help me clarify my career goals so I can make the greatest contribution. I really appreciate that.

In your letter of inquiry, remember to (1) begin directly with your question, (2) add the briefest information about yourself the reader needs to help you, (3) ask specific questions so the reader doesn't need to think what you might want to know, and (4) be grateful for the assistance. Work on retaining a you-attitude.

RIDE-ALONG PROGRAMS

Many companies are happy to have you spend a day going with the person who holds the job you think you might like. In the language of human resource management, this is a "realistic job preview." You get a chance to see what the jobholder *really* does by observing firsthand. The benefit to you is obvious: you are much more likely to apply for jobs you love. The company also benefits. It ends up with employees who *know* they will like the work so are much more likely to stay.

For example, most police departments have a ride-along program. You can spend a shift with a police officer watching what happens: how much paperwork is involved, how much time is spent alone, how much time is spent with others, how many policies and procedures must be followed, how happy the officer appears to be with the different tasks, and so on.

Rotary International has a program called Academics Build Choice. A specific part of the program involves students in ride-along experiences. The students all submit two job types that interest them. Members of Rotary who hold those jobs take the students along for a day of work.

Almost all companies are willing to arrange a ride-along day for you. You need only ask. Sometimes you must sign an insurance waiver.

As Arnold Glasow said, "In life, as in football, you won't go far unless you know where the goal posts are." Clarifying your job-hunting goals is the most important, and first, step.

MAKING A PLAN

Once you feel relatively confident about your goals, about where you want to end up, you need a plan for getting there. The first step is to assess clearly where you are right now.

Identifying Your Qualifications

Begin writing down all the pieces of your background that have contributed to making you the person you are. Where have you lived? What schools have you attended? What have you studied? What do you do for fun?

While you are doing this exercise, don't worry about whether the information is directly (or even indirectly) job related. The important part of this step is to get all the information down.

Because at least some of this information will ultimately be used in the preparation of your résumé, you will find it particularly helpful to write **each piece** of background information on a **different** small notecard. That will allow you to sort the different experiences into *types* of information— formal education, work experience, hobbies, and so on. It will also allow you to rank order them easily in terms of personal satisfaction, job relevance, or chronological order.

Here are some topics that will help you think about your life, what you've done, and what you like to do. Write down the answers. Be as complete as possible.

Exercise 10.2

Formal education:
  Where did you go to school?
  When?
  What did you study?
  What kinds of major projects did you complete? Do you still have any of them?

Did you do any independent studies? What? Why?

What kinds of grades did you get?

What degrees do you have?

Other education:

Have you taken any workshops? When? What?

Do you use a computer? What? How Much?

Do you type? How fast?

Do you take shorthand? How fast?

What languages do you know? How well—read, write, converse?

Do you know any specialized professional languages—law, medicine?

Certifications:

Are you formally certified to do anything—CPR, SCUBA diving, water safety, CPA, CMA, CPM, private airplane pilot, truck driver's license?

Work experience:

What jobs have you held? When? Where?

What tasks do you feel competent handling?

Have you managed: people? things? information? ideas?

Were you paid? How much?

Have you been fired? Why?

Military experience:

Have you been in the military? Branch? Time? Grade?

Where did you serve? Do you have war experience?

Life experience:

Where are all the places you've lived? For how long? When?

How many children do you have? How old?

Are you married?

How is your health? Have you been hospitalized?

Are you active in a church or religion?

Are you active in a political party?

Have you ever been arrested? Spent time in jail?

Have you ever sued anyone or been sued?

Did your family have a lot or a little money when you were growing up?

Interests:

Sports? Do you compete formally?

Hobbies? Have you ever had a showing, entered a fair?
Leisure activities? Do you have season tickets?
Musical instruments? Do you belong to a group?

Club memberships:
　　Civic organizations?
　　School organizations?
　　Fraternities/sororities?
　　Honorary?
　　Church/religious?
　　Professional?
　　Personal interest?

Regular reading:
　　Newspapers?
　　Magazines?
　　Journals?

Awards and honors:
　　School?
　　Civic?
　　Professional?
　　Military?

Anything else that makes you who you are.

Identifying the Job Requirements

Based on your research of the kinds of jobs that interest you, make a list of the qualifications the jobs require. What kind of educational and experiential background is required? What experiences or skills are preferred? What personal qualities do people who hold these jobs have?

Setting the Plan

Once you have the list of your background skills and qualifications and the list of the requirements for the jobs you are considering, you are ready to determine what needs to be done. You may find you need some additional education. You may want to join a professional organization and make some personal contacts. Perhaps a certification exam is required. Once you know what needs to be done, you will have a clearer idea of how to do it and how long it will take.

As John-Roger and Peter McWilliams say in their 1992 book, *Wealth 101*, "Plans are funny things: without them, we seldom get to our goal. When we've gotten to our goal, however, we look back and realize we haven't gotten there according to our plan." Perhaps the final word on plans and planning is the need for flexibility. A plan is a good, maybe even necessary thing. On the other hand, circumstances and conditions change. Be willing to adapt.

BEGINNING THE JOB SEARCH

When you are prepared to begin the actual process of applying for specific positions, several tasks await you. The first is identifying jobs to apply for. Several steps are involved.

Network

Perhaps the most important step in finding the right job is to enlist the help of others. The saying "It's not what you know but who you know" has relevance in the search process. The more people who know you are seeking employment, the better. Frequently businesspeople ask their acquaintances if they know any talented people who might be looking for work. Obviously it's to your advantage to be part of a network of contacts who will suggest your name.

You can build your network by incorporating some of the following ideas.

Broaden your circle of friends: Join Toastmasters or a community organization. Attend Chamber of Commerce meetings and talk with people. Seek out people you don't know at social gatherings.

Get to know your professors: Perform well in their classes; visit them during office hours; ask them to keep you in mind if they hear of any job opportunities.

Meet business executives: Join a professional organization in your field (like IEEE for engineers, NAA for accountants, or APICS for manufacturing managers). Go on factory tours; talk with guest speakers in classes; write to people you admire.

Let family and friends know you are looking for employment. Make sure they know what kinds of work interest you. Try to get the word out across a wide geographical area.

Look for Potential Employers

You can apply to any organization for work. However, if an organization has advertised an opening, your application will be much easier because you know they need someone, the contact person's name, the qualifications being sought, deadlines, salary range, and other helpful information. You can tailor your résumé and job application letter to fit the position you are applying for.

If you do not know whether a company is seeking employees, you can apply anyway. You would think about your résumé and job application letter as if they were persuasive messages sent to cold prospects. You would need to include slightly more information in the beginning to explain why you are writing. An excellent alternative is to take your résumé and visit in person the company where you wish to work. The placement office of a company usually knows about positions that will be available before those positions are advertised.

Many sources offer information on advertised job openings. Consider using some or all of the following:

- newspaper classified advertisements
- university placement centers
- your network of friends and family
- employment agencies—both state-supported and private companies
- publications in your field
- on-line data bases such as Prodigy or computer bulletin boards
- the placement office of the company you work for

Armed with a job announcement, you are ready to begin the next steps in the job-hunting process. In the next chapters, we will discuss résumé preparation and job application letter writing.

*D*eciding what career path will best suit you requires that you know two things. First, you need to know what people who hold certain jobs actually do and what background, personal qualities, and skills are used in those jobs. You can research the answers indirectly by using library sources, or you can ask and observe people who are currently performing those jobs.

Second, you need to know about yourself. What skills, interests, personal qualities, and background experiences do you have? Self-analysis is called for here.

Once you have these two pieces of information, you can develop a plan for achieving your career goals. The more you know about yourself and the jobs you are interested in, the greater your chance of securing employment you love. Your knowledge will reduce your tension. It will also allow you to tailor your job application materials so they put your strongest qualities forward.

The last step before you actually begin preparing your résumé and job application letter is to find advertised job openings. Although you can send your job application to any organization, responding to a job announcement is much easier. Once you have the information on open positions, you are ready to begin putting pen to paper.

11

The Résumé

Once you have completed the exercises in Chapter 10, you are ready to begin the development of your application materials. Although it is usually the second piece of writing a potential employer sees about you, the résumé is the first document you prepare.

A résumé highlights your achievements and begins to tell the story of why you are the perfect person for the job you are seeking. In this chapter, we will discuss résumés—how they are used, why we prepare them with such care, and how to prepare the kind of résumé that will help you get an interview.

AN OVERVIEW OF THE RÉSUMÉ

A résumé is sometimes called a *data sheet, dossier,* or *vitae*. It introduces you, providing the reader with a **summary of your qualifications** for the job. It includes all the background information you think the reader should have about you.

Résumés are designed for quick reading. Rather than complete sentences and detailed descriptions of your qualifications, the résumé uses lists, fragments, bulleted points. The résumé also uses format, typeface, and color to draw attention to significant points.

Many companies require job applicants to fill out standardized application forms. The standard application form does not allow you to highlight or bring attention to the qualities which you believe to be your strengths. Résumés do. As a result, even when you are asked to submit a completed application form, it is a wise idea to attach your résumé as well.

Apply Persuasive Techniques

To design the most effective résumé, you need to follow the principles of persuasion. Excellent salespeople begin with a thorough knowledge of the product and as much knowledge of the customer as they can reasonably obtain. Since you are the product, the more you know about your strengths and weaknesses for the position you are applying for, the better.

You must also have information about the "customer." As we discussed in the last chapter, applying for an advertised position is easier than prospecting. The announcement will tell you about the qualifications the employer is seeking. Your job will be to indicate how you meet them. When you are not applying for an announced position, you will need to use logic to make an educated guess about the qualities the company is looking for.

Research the Company

In either case, you will do a better job of preparing your résumé (and job application letter) if you know something about the company you are applying to. Companies have personalities. Each has its own culture that reflects the biases and expectations of the original owners, modified by all the people who have been a part of the company. Some companies value competition and competitiveness. They look for those qualities in every employee they hire, regardless of the specific job.

Other companies value flexibility and the ability to change rapidly. They might anticipate moving employees frequently, from town to town and job to job. Potential employees who have lived in several states or countries may look like better job candidates to such companies than candidates who have lived only in one town.

Knowing the company's culture is obviously important to your persuasive effort. You can find out about a corporation's culture by reading materials the company has published and reading articles about the company.

INFORMATION PREPARED BY THE COMPANY

The annual report to the stockholders is an excellent place to begin your research. Notice what the company includes in its report in addition to the legally required financial disclosures. What pictures are included? What are the people in the pictures doing? What are they wearing? Is the company unionized? How are its relations with its employees? Are any lawsuits pending against the company? How old are the corporate officers? What kinds of backgrounds do the officers have? Have they been with the company long? Annual reports are often available in your local library. You can also obtain one by writing to the company.

You might also consider the company's advertisements. Does it use print media, radio, television? How does it portray its products? How does it portray the people who appear in its advertisements? Is the focus on quality, price, usefulness, emotion? Do you believe the advertisements are honest and accurate?

Does the company publish a newsletter for its employees? If so, you can learn a great deal about the corporate culture by reading several issues. You can easily obtain copies of company newsletters by calling or writing to the personnel or human resource department of the company and asking for them.

If the company is unionized, write or call the union which would represent you if you got the job and ask for any information on working conditions they believe you should have. They will be eager to help you.

INFORMATION PREPARED BY OTHERS

All the large corporations and many of the small ones are written about in business journals and magazines. The *Business Periodicals Index*, which is in the reference section of your library, lists all the recent articles about a firm under the firm's name. Read those your library has available, or write to the publication that printed the article and ask for a copy of it.

If you are interested in working for a smaller firm, the local newspaper is certain to have articles on it. Newspapers have indexes of such articles. Once again, look under the firm's name in the index; then look up the article in the newspaper's archives.

Spend the Necessary Time

You might be sensing that the process of job hunting is time-consuming. It is. As we observed in Chapter 10, finding and obtaining the best job for you is a job in itself. The results are worth the effort. Obviously a job candidate who has carefully researched potential jobs, the companies who hire people to do those jobs, and his or her qualities is in a much better position to put together a persuasive package of materials than one who is merely "sending out applications."

Sometimes it is helpful to think of the resistance to hiring you. To begin with, you are a very expensive product. You can imagine how much price resistance you would have to overcome to spend $30,000 on a BMW automobile. You might imagine all the alternative ways you could use that money.

As a job applicant, suppose you are looking for a job that pays you $30,000. Of course, with you, it isn't a one-time payment—you will want another $30,000 next year (plus a raise). You will probably anticipate a benefits package worth approximately one-third of your annual income. And a training program would be nice. The average large company figures it will spend $100,000 on your training over the first three years.

Needless to say, you are an expensive product. You will need to overcome a great deal of price resistance. And the company will have many alternative products to choose from. Your persuasive skills will be put to the test. The need for excellent product and customer information is obvious. You will need to spend whatever time is required to obtain it.

THE ELEMENTS OF A RÉSUMÉ

Most résumés include the same general categories of information. The major categories **always** found on a résumé include the following:

- your name, address, and phone number
- your educational background
- your experience as it relates to the position you are applying for

Other categories which are frequently found on résumés include the following:

- job objective (or the position you are applying for)
- awards and honors
- interests and hobbies
- memberships
- computer skills
- language skills
- management skills
- references
- volunteer work
- publications
- presentations

The general principle is to have a logical reason for everything you include and for everything you don't include. For example, if you are in the top 20 percent of students in your class, you might want to say so. If you are in the bottom 20 percent, don't include the information. If your grades are important to a particular company or for a particular job, they will request an official copy of your transcripts anyway.

Many companies prefer applicants to limit their résumé to one page. If you are relatively new to the job market—for example, a recent college graduate who went to college right after high school—the one-page limit makes sense. It will force you to think carefully about what information is really important and will keep you from becoming wordy.

If you have been in the work force for fifteen years, the one-page limit will not make sense, and you should not feel compelled to follow it. As long as you remember the résumé is to highlight your accomplishments, make your résumé as long as you need to. You might consider these alternatives to the multiple-page, stapled résumé.

- Have both sides of the paper printed (be sure to write "please see over" on **both** sides of the résumé if you do this).
- Use legal-size paper and fold it so you have a flap on an 8 1/2 x 11 paper (this version gives you a little more room and a nice place for your name and address).
- Use the portfolio approach and put your résumé in a binder. Include newspaper clippings about you, copies of your awards, copies of papers you've written. Models use this format and include proofs of advertisements they have appeared in. Artists use this format and include samples of their work and programs of shows their work has appeared in. The portfolio approach can easily be adapted for engineers, computer programmers, and many others. (Before you choose this approach, remember that the company will probably make copies of just the résumé portion of your portfolio which will be circulated to those who make the hiring decision. As a result, the résumé portion must be strong enough to stand alone.)

Arranging the Information

Different candidates applying for different jobs in different organizations will require different arrangements of information. In general, apply the communication principle **first and last are positions of emphasis**. If your education is what makes you a strong candidate, put your education first. If your experience is what gives you the edge, put your experience first.

Within any entry, apply the principle of first and last again. Don't put the dates of your employment first—that isn't what you want to emphasize. Instead put your job title first. Again, apply logic and do what will help you the most.

Usually the job title would go first. However, suppose two summers ago you had a summer job at Intel. Now you want to apply for a full-time, career position there. In that case, you might want to give emphasis to the fact that you have worked at Intel before, so you would put the names of the companies where you worked first, in the position of emphasis.

Grammatical Parallelism

Once you have established the order for presenting your information, stick with it. If in the experience section you present your most recent job in the order: job title, place of work, dates of employment, duties, and skills demonstrated, present all your work experience in the same order.

Example 11.1

Head Nurse. Good Samaritan Hospital, Phoenix, AZ. 1990–present.
Duties: Schedule and supervise work of seventeen nurses on 23-bed
ward. Skills demonstrated: Excellent communication skills. Ability to
work well with doctors, nurses, orderlies, and patients. Won Top
Employee honors for work on bringing quality management principles into health care.

Job Title. Place of employment, city, state. Dates worked.
Duties: Skills demonstrated:

If you are still doing the job, use the present tense. If you no longer
perform the job, use the past tense. If you are presenting a list of skills,
duties, or qualities, make sure that all the entries in the list are grammatically parallel. If your first entry begins with a verb, begin all your entries
with a verb. If you use gerunds, use the gerund form throughout. The following two examples demonstrate the correct use of grammatical parallelism. Note that the underlined words are all in similar grammatical
form.

Example 11.2A

Duties:
> <u>prepared</u> daily account summaries
> <u>trained</u> four new employees
> <u>developed</u> the filing system now used by entire company
> <u>kept</u> mailing list up to date
> <u>computerized</u> mailing list

Example 11.2B

Duties included:
> <u>preparing</u> daily account summaries
> <u>training</u> four new employees
> <u>developing</u> the filing system now used companywide
> <u>keeping</u> mailing list current
> <u>computerizing</u> mailing list

Reversing Chronological Order

Almost always, education and experience are presented in **reverse
chronological order**. That means your most recent degree or job goes first,
followed by the one immediately prior, and so on back to your first. The
logic of this order is that *usually* an applicant's most recent job is the one
with the most responsibility and pay.

There are situations where your most recent job is not your best experience. For example, suppose you were working as a purchasing agent for a

large company. You decided to quit and get a master's degree in manufacturing management. You worked evenings as a waiter in a dinner restaurant. Your job as waiter is not as relevant to your application for the position of inventory control manager as your purchasing agent job was.

If in your situation the logic of reverse chronological order doesn't hold, consider making a special heading like **Education and Experience Directly Related to Inventory Control** and another heading like **Other Education and Experience.** Within each category, you can use the expected reverse chronological order and still have your most important experience first.

Using Headings

Even though résumés are short, usually one page, the different categories of information are given headings. The overall document is also titled. Type **RÉSUMÉ** at the top; then your name, address, and phone number. You might also choose to title your résumé with a more informational title: **résumé of CHARLES NUGYEN HOLT.** An even more informational alternative would be: **Qualifications of CHARLES NUGYEN HOLT for the position of Labor Relations Chief Negotiator**.

Then add a heading or title for each grouping of information. Choose a heading that most highlights the kinds of information you are going to include. You can be quite creative with your titles. You don't have to group your information in any set way.

GRAPHIC DESIGN

If your company was going to change its entire corporate image and wanted to support the change with new logo, letterhead, and business forms, you would probably seek advice from a graphic-design expert. Because the visual communication of a résumé is such a powerful communicator of your professional competence, you might want to get professional advice on your résumé's graphic design. A professional graphic-design artist will help you decide on the most visually pleasing arrangement of information, typeface and size, paper, color, and perhaps even a logo or personal mark.

Assuming that consulting a graphic-design artist is not an option, here are some of the things to think about as you put together the visual elements of your résumé.

HEADINGS

Make the headings darker and larger than the type you use for your information. You will want them to stand out. They help your reader interpret the information.

You might include some color in your headings. You could have the headings printed in color. The most frequently used color on résumés is blue. An alternative would be to type your headings in black; then underline them in red.

In general, headings should appear to be more important than the information under them. On the other hand, you will not want the heading to overwhelm the important information about you, so your goal is to choose type, size, and color that are visually pleasing and show the relative importance of the information.

You can center your headings, have them further to the left than the rest of your information, even have them right-justified. The goal is to draw attention to the résumé without drawing attention from the information.

VISUAL BALANCE

When a reader picks up your résumé, you want it to look well balanced. The page should appear full but not crowded. Information on the left should be balanced by information on the right. The top margin should be slightly larger than the bottom margin. The overall sense of the document should be a well-framed picture.

Dark, bold headings will take up more "visual space" than words in small type. As a result, to make your picture balanced, you will need many words in small type to balance a single word in large type.

Framing information in white space draws attention to it, so you might want to indent the most important information from both the left and right sides. The extra margin will emphasize the information and retain your visual balance.

TYPE

The most important advice about type is make it dark and clear. Typing your résumé on an old typewriter using a worn ribbon will send many messages about you, none of which you probably want sent. The first is that you don't care very much about the quality of your work. The second is that you do not have computer skills. The third is that you don't know any better (you don't know what professional work looks like).

Of course, you may have very good reasons for your use of a worn ribbon. You just heard about this job which has an application deadline this afternoon. You think this would be the perfect job. Your computer is in the repair shop. The only machine available to you is your old typewriter. You've just got to get this application in. So actually, the use of the old machine means you <u>really</u> care. Unfortunately, that just isn't the way your nonverbals will be interpreted.

PAPER

The quality and color of paper is also an important consideration in your overall design. Use 24-pound bond paper. Many companies refer to this paper as résumé bond. The greater the rag or cotton-fiber content, the better. Twenty-five percent rag content would be minimal. Best would be 100 percent cotton-fiber paper.

White is the most conservative color for résumés and is appropriate when you are applying for conservative positions such as loan officer, financial advisor, or public accountant. You might also want to use white paper when you are applying to a company with a conservative corporate culture, no matter what position you are applying for.

Light grays, creams, or blues are also appropriate for résumés. One applicant applying to Mary Kay Cosmetics, put her résumé on light pink, the company's trademark color. If you are applying for a position in one of the creative arts—for example, advertising or graphic design—you might consider a bolder, less conservative paper type or color. You would be allowing the nonverbal elements of your résumé to speak for you, saying you are more creative, bolder, less conventional.

Whichever paper you choose, remember the goal. You want the visual elements of your résumé to draw attention to but not overwhelm or detract from the important information about you.

PHRASING THE INFORMATION

You want to highlight what is best about your background. Several techniques will assist you to do that. Perhaps the most important is to use action verbs. Stress what you have <u>done</u> and what you are <u>doing</u>.

Focus on Activity

Employers, especially of college graduates, are wary of job applicants who know <u>what</u> but not <u>how</u>. They want to hire people who are doers, people who get the job done. Focus on activity. Use action verbs. The following is a list of some verbs you might consider incorporating into your work experience or educational information:

created	developed	trained
achieved	identified	computerized
analyzed	evaluated	achieved
designed	wrote	presented
negotiated	coordinated	managed
planned	implemented	generated

Use Specific Facts

A résumé that provides specific detail is more powerful than one that makes general statements. For example, "supervised a crew of ten" is better than "was crew supervisor." "Reduced departmental overhead by 23%" is more powerful than "was responsible for reducing overhead." "Generated $92,000 in new sales" and "negotiated savings of 16% on inventory of over 3,000 parts" are nicely specific.

Being specific is better, even when your accomplishments are comparatively minor. For example, "responsible for balancing cash drawer averaging $230" is significantly better than "was responsible for balancing own cash drawer," even though the amount entrusted to the employee was small.

Use Sentence Fragments

Very few résumés use complete sentences. None of the really good ones do. The goal of the résumé is to provide highlights of your qualifications that can be read rapidly. Fragments read faster than complete sentences, as any advertising copy writer can tell you.

In addition to speeding up the reading process, fragments allow you to step out of the picture. The word *I* is simply not used—ever. Since every piece of information on the résumé is about you, *I* would be redundant. It would also be irritating, making the document sound overwhelmingly "I-attitude."

Avoid Personal Information

The law makes it illegal for an organization to discriminate in hiring on the basis of age, sex, race, color, creed, religion, country of origin, or handicaps. Organizations are justifiably nervous about being accused of breaking the antidiscrimination laws. Unless the information can be shown to be a necessary element of doing the job, companies would rather not even have the information.

Unless you know the employer specifically needs the information, **do not include personal information**. The employer does not need to know if you are male or female, a parent or not, black or white, Catholic or Jewish.

On the other hand, if you are going to serve alcohol, you must be old enough to do so legally, so you may say "over 21" (or whatever the legal age to serve alcohol is in the state you are applying to work in). If you suspect the company will move you around in the next four years, you can say "free to relocate." Don't say "single."

Proofread

The job application letter and résumé are often the only information a company's officers have about you while they are making the decision to offer you an interview. As a result, they are assuming these pieces of work represent all your work—the way you go about things. Errors of grammar or proofreading are deadly. Your application package must be perfect.

Proofreading is difficult. We often see what we expect to be on the page rather than what is on the page. You will need help from friends. Use the spelling checker on your computer. Read backward from the bottom of your résumé to the top, looking at each word. Then check again.

And then ask another person to check for you. Your résumé must be perfect!

Highlight Transferable Skills

When covering work experience, at a minimum you need to include dates, places, firms, and duties. For education, include institutions, dates, degrees, and areas of study. These data are required elements of a résumé. They are not, however, what will get you the job.

You need to highlight the skills you have developed which you can now bring to your new employer. Provide evidence that you can work well with others, work unsupervised, do quality work, communicate well, learn quickly, remain organized, work under stress, and so on. What are the skills you will need in the new position? Try to provide evidence that your background has developed those skills in you.

When you are applying for a job directly related to a job you have held before, focusing on your duties—what you specifically did—will help you. When you are changing careers or just starting one, focusing on your transferable skills will give you the edge. A counterperson at McDonald's learns to work quickly, accurately, and with good interpersonal skills. Those skills will help a recent college graduate who wants an auditing job with Price Waterhouse. Working on the family farm in the summer teaches people to work under challenging physical conditions, to work alone and unsupervised, to work safely around heavy equipment. Those same skills can be used by a manufacturing manager or a forester. Stress the skills you have developed.

COMPARE RÉSUMÉS

Most business communication books include four or five sample résumés. However, the paper quality, type quality, and colors of the original are lost in the text. As a result, the reader doesn't get the full effect of a model résumé. You do not see what your actual competition looks like.

The fastest way to learn what works well in résumés is to look at a large number of them. Whenever you apply for a position, the chances are that your résumé will appear in a stack of résumés. What will make yours stand out? The best way to answer that question is to look at a stack of résumés and see which ones stand out to you. Then use those as models for yours.

Your school placement center typically has files or binders of résumés.

Sometimes they are divided into career types. The business majors will be in a binder separate from those for the education majors or the graphic arts majors. Look at them all.

Local graphic artists keep binders of résumés that display their work. Visit two or three. If you have a friend in business who will let you look at some résumés on file, that would be excellent. Take every opportunity to look at as many résumés as you can.

Notice what makes you like one more than another. Pay attention to typeface, paper quality, and color. What kinds of headings are used? What information is included? Do you prefer a particular way of phrasing information? Do the résumés you like have borders or graphics?

Choose strong elements from those you like and build your résumé around those. Making up your own model based on looking at many résumés is much better than copying a model from a text.

The résumé is prepared before other application materials. It is a sort of billboard highlighting the experiences in your background that make you an excellent potential employee.

The résumé advertises your accomplishments. It serves as your ambassador, introducing you to potential employers. Therefore, it requires special attention. Both what you say and how you say it are important. Four principles will assist you in creating the perfect résumé. First, remember that first and last are positions of emphasis. Put your most relevant information there.

Second, have a logical reason for everything you include and everything you don't include. Each person's résumé will be different. Don't just blindly follow the format someone else has used.

Third, use grammatically parallel phrases and sentence fragments rather than full sentences. Avoid the use of I. *Last, make your résumé look good—well balanced and attractive.*

12

Job Application Letters

In the last chapter, we discussed the contents of a résumé and determined that the effective résumé highlights those aspects of your background that make you a qualified candidate. In this chapter, we will discuss the job application letter.

A job application letter takes the place of the résumé or, more frequently, is sent along with your résumé. The application letter shows the reader specifically how you will put what you know to work for the new employer.

A job application letter is a modified version of the sales or persuasive strategy we practiced in Chapter 8. In this chapter, we will learn how to apply the persuasive message strategy to the marketing of ourselves.

THE JOB APPLICATION LETTER

A job application letter, sometimes called a *cover letter*, is the tool you use to formally apply for a job. Except in highly unusual situations, the letter uses the persuasive message strategy. The action you want the reader to take is to offer you an interview—to give you the opportunity to sell yourself in person.

Either the résumé and job application letter are sent together, or the job application letter stands alone. When the letter is sent alone, it must include more specific details. Job application letters can be sent in response to an advertised position, or you can use them to determine if a company has openings in your job area. Each situation requires a slightly different approach, so we'll address them individually.

In all cases, the job application letter includes the following:

- a clear request to be considered for a specific job
- evidence that you meet the qualifications for doing the job
- a request for an interview

The job application letter is probably the most important single piece of writing a business writer prepares. You must think of it as your only chance to make an excellent impression on the decision makers in a company.

When a company advertises a job opening, it hopes to receive many applications. The larger the pool of applicants the company has to choose from, the more likely it will find the right person for the position.

The Search for Negative Information

When company decision makers are faced with limited time and many applications, research shows that they approach the decision-making process by looking for negative information. They are looking for reasons to put your application in the "Do not consider further" pile. As a result, your letter must look professional and be easy to read. You must *demonstrate* your communication competence. Any proofreading or spelling errors will be used to disqualify your application.

The focus on negative news may seem unfair, especially if the job you are applying for does not require you to have excellent writing skills. Fair or unfair, it is easier to succeed if you understand what is being asked of you.

Preparing to Write the Letter

As with all communication situations, audience analysis is a critical first step in preparing your job application letter. Here are some things you know about your audience before you even begin to research the specific company.

YOUR AUDIENCE

Your audience wants to hear from you. Whether a company has advertised a position or not, it is pleased to have many qualified applicants applying for jobs. As a result, your attention-getting beginning is relatively easy to craft. Just saying you wish to be considered for a particular position will capture the reader's attention.

Your audience is very busy. The more ideal the company and the job, the more applications the company is likely to receive. In other words, the more you want the job, the more others are likely to want it. Your reader will have a great deal to do. Do not waste the reader's time. Make your points clearly and rapidly. Use short sentences. Arrange them in short paragraphs.

Your audience wants to choose the best candidate. The reader will be looking for *evidence* that you meet the qualifications. Rather than making statements that you have the required skills, provide evidence that you do. Here are some examples:

Example 12.1

Assertion: I am a quick learner.
Assertion with evidence: My GPA and graduation with honors attest to the fact that I am an excellent learner.

Assertion: My interpersonal skills are strong and will allow me to be a great sales representative.
Assertion with evidence: As fund-raiser for my fraternity, I demonstrated my ability to call upon local business managers and convince them to donate their products to support a worthy cause.

Assertion: I enjoy working with people and am a good team player.
Assertion with evidence: In addition to my regular schoolwork and part-time job, I play soccer on an intramural team. I was elected captain of the team twice, which I believe attests to my teamwork skills.

Assertion: Even though I have only two years of experience, I am confident that I can handle the tasks of the job as well as someone who has had five years of experience.
Assertion with evidence: As my résumé indicates, I have only two years of work experience in this field. However, I have now earned a bachelor's degree and completed a seven-month internship with one of the most innovative organizations in the industry. I believe my combination of experience and education is an excellent alternative to five years of experience.

Assertion: I have excellent written communication skills.
Assertion with evidence: (Just demonstrate your competence.)

Once you choose a position to apply for and an organization to apply to, you can add specific information to what you know about your audience. You can consider the organizational climate; the age, sex, and position of the person you are writing to; and any other information you have.

READER BENEFIT, YOU-ATTITUDE, AND *I*

A job application letter, like any sales letter, must focus on benefits the reader will receive from doing what the writer wants. Using you-attitude and avoiding an "I want" focus is important. However, it is important to understand the difference between use of the word *I* and "I-attitude." Suppose you were writing to a potential customer and you hoped to persuade that customer to buy your brand of closet-organizing shelving. If the name of your product was Core Closets, you would assume that you could develop good reader benefit and use you-attitude while also stating the name of your product frequently. Here's an example of a paragraph from such a letter:

Example 12.2

> With a Core Closet system installed, you will be able to find your favorite belt. Your shirts will retain their fresh-pressed look. Core Closets can even help your expensive shoes last longer by providing proper airing and storing.

In job application letters, the name of the product is *I*. As a result, you will need to use *I* in your letter. As long as you retain reader benefit and a good you-attitude, using the name of your product is expected. The only warning is that if you have a tendency toward I-attitude *and* the name of your product is *I,* your tone can easily become overbearing and self-centered. Here's an example of incorporating reader benefit, you-attitude, and the *I* product name.

Example 12.3

> Your job announcement indicates you are looking for a candidate with strong interpersonal skills. Over the last three summers, I have worked as a tour guide for the Detroit Chamber of Commerce. In that position, I developed my abilities to help a great variety of people enjoy themselves in a strange environment.
>
> I did that by listening carefully to their questions and by taking an interest in them: where they came from and why they were visiting Detroit. Last summer, the chamber members honored me with a luncheon to celebrate my 100th tour. I believe these same communication skills will serve me well as a member of your management consulting team.

APPROPRIATE TONE

Perhaps the most difficult part of writing a perfect job application letter is achieving the perfect tone. One the one hand, you need to **sound confident**. You are convinced you can do the job. You have the skills. You can learn. You can communicate. Actually, this company would be foolish not to offer you the position.

On the other hand, your tone needs to indicate that you are not pushy, not a show-off, not a know-it-all. Your tone must reflect your awareness that the person who is reviewing your application has higher status than you do. Although confident, you understand that all the **decision-making power lies with the reader**. You can ask to be interviewed. You cannot demand it nor even expect it.

These two opposing forces create a tightrope balancing act. You must remain on that very fine line between confidence and overconfidence. In general, the best ways to handle this problem are to

- provide specific evidence for each of your claims
- be polite
- ask rather than tell.

THE ADVERTISED JOB

Because of some important differences between the job application letter to apply for an *advertised* opening and the *prospecting* application letter, we'll address each separately.

When you have a position announcement, your letter has been pretty well outlined for you. Most position announcements include a list of what the company believes are minimum qualifications. In your letter, you provide evidence that you meet all the qualifications. (Sometimes you have alternative qualifications that you believe are adequate or even superior substitutions.)

Here is the strategy for writing an application letter when you have an announced opening:

I. In the first paragraph, state specifically that you wish to be considered for the position. Here are some sample opening paragraphs.

Please consider my application for the position of sales representative which you advertised in the *Daily Gazette*.

You listed an internship position with the State University placement office. Please consider my qualifications for the position.

The background experience you are seeking in an applicant for your purchasing manager position matches mine very closely. Please consider my application for the job.

All these beginnings accomplish several goals. They:

- use you-attitude.
- refer to the advertised position.
- specifically ask to be considered for the position.

II. In the middle paragraphs of the letter, refer to a qualification listed in the advertisement and explain by providing evidence how you meet the qualification. Continue until you have covered at least a majority of the specified qualifications. (This is the equivalent in the persuasive message strategy of identifying a need and then showing how your product—you—meets the need. In the case of an advertised position, the company has done the work of identifying its needs for you.) Here are some examples of this approach of "need" followed by "evidence of meeting need":

Example 12.4

You indicated that you were looking for a person with at least five years experience in warehousing and warehouse management. As my résumé details, I have worked for K-Mart at their warehouse and shipping center in Reno, Nevada, for the last seven years. During my first two years, I worked on the warehouse floor preparing shipments. I was then promoted to supervisor, managing a team of twelve. The company showed its faith in my management skills by giving me the shift manager's position after only fourteen months as supervisor. I held that position until I quit to attend graduate school.

The position of sales representative requires excellent people skills. I developed my interpersonal skills as a customer service representative for Federal Express. Working at the Atlanta airport gave me the opportunity to observe the best customer-service people in the business. I believe my Employee of the Month award is testimony to the fact that I learned what they had to teach me.

Your announcement indicated you need someone fluent in Spanish. In addition to four years of college-level Spanish, I lived in Peru for seven months. That experience allowed me to go from competent reading and writing of Spanish to conversational fluency. In addition to polishing my language skills, I also learned a great deal about the Latin culture.

Continue with this approach until you have specifically addressed more than half the stated qualifications. When you have completed that, you can refer the reader to your résumé for more information on your background. Here are some examples of how to do that:

Example 12.5

My résumé provides additional evidence of my qualifications for this position.

As the enclosed résumé indicates, I have also contributed to my community through volunteer work.

I believe my résumé provides support for my assertion that my background uniquely qualifies me for this position.

As my résumé details, I have the experience and the education that makes me confident that I can do exceptional work for you.

III. In the final paragraph, ask confidently and politely for an interview.

The last paragraph of a persuasive message should call for action. The action you want the reader to take is to allow you the opportunity to speak in person. In Chapter 8, we learned to make taking action easy, to end-date when possible, and to justify any end-date you use. Here are some examples of ending call-for-action paragraphs:

Example 12.6

> Should you agree that my background and experience match your needs, I would appreciate the opportunity to talk with you in person. I can be reached at (788) 545-6220 Monday-Thursday, or you may leave a message, and I will get right back to you.

> Could we arrange an interview? At that time I would be delighted to discuss with you how I could make a contribution to AxeAll.

> I will be in Biloxi between March 3 and March 9. Would a time during that week be convenient?

> My education and experience are detailed on my résumé. My interpersonal skills are best communicated face-to-face. I would appreciate the opportunity of an interview. A phone call to (668) 342-1676 will bring me at your convenience to demonstrate my abilities to contribute to Intrepid.

As with all call-for-action endings, once you have stated the action you want the reader to take, stop. Avoid tagging anything else on the end of your letter.

In general, you will find that job application letters are like sales letters. They are longer than letters following other strategies. The reader will have some built-in resistance to your desired action. The letter needs to be long enough to overcome the reader's resistance. Job application letters are typically a full page or more in length. Remember, this letter and your résumé may provide the only chance you have to talk an organization into hiring you. Make the letter long enough to do the job.

THE PROSPECTING JOB APPLICATION LETTER

Some companies do not advertise their job openings. There can be many reasons for this. The least pleasant (and largely illegal) reason is that they want to discriminate toward or against a particular group of applicants. They can let a carefully selected grapevine of people know they may be hiring, thus controlling the applicant pool.

Another reason for not advertising openings is that management believes it has enough unsolicited applications. IBM, Hewlett-Packard, Apple, and Intel frequently fall in this category.

Sometimes positions aren't advertised because there isn't time. A replacement is needed right away. Or a prospecting job applicant makes an application just as a position becomes open, and the applicant is offered the job before it is officially vacant.

In these and other cases, you may succeed in obtaining a job without knowing whether a position is open. To be successful at this type of prospecting job application letter, modify the overall persuasive message strategy in the following ways.

I. In the first paragraph, you may need to be more attention getting than in the solicited application letter. If someone who works at the organization you are applying to suggested you apply, use that as your attention-getting beginning. Typically, organizations would rather hire someone somebody knows. Here is an example of that sort of beginning:

Example 12.7

> Mary Gomez, of your marketing staff, suggested that you might be hiring sales trainees in the next month or two. Please consider my qualifications for that position.

In Chapter 8, we discussed the power of the question for gaining the reader's attention. You can use the attention-getting question in a job application letter:

Example 12.8

> In what ways might your organization benefit from knowledge of the latest in quality-management techniques? Improved customer service, faster new-product development, and improved worker morale are typical outcomes of quality-management programs. Please consider my qualifications for bringing these and other benefits to your manufacturing facility.

If you are applying to anything other than a very conservative company, you can even use color and boldface type to grab your reader's attention:

Reduced inventory.
Improved on-time delivery.
Increased profits.

> Let me help you achieve these results. Please consider my application for a purchasing manager position.

Notice that even though you do not know whether such a position exists, you write as if one did. You specifically identify the position you wish to be considered for. Some job hunters resist this advice. Their logic tells them to explain their qualifications and then ask if there is a position where those qualities could be applied. Research demonstrates emphatically that decision makers want job applicants to apply for specific positions. If the company likes your qualifications but sees you in a different role than the one you applied for, it will ask you to consider interviewing for the alternative position. An organization is not going to let a talented applicant go because the applicant asked to be considered for a position that is not available. Apply specifically.

II. In your middle paragraphs, follow the same pattern as in the letter of application for an advertised position—need, evidence of meeting need. The difference is that you will need to *imagine* reader need rather than having the position announcement tell you what qualifications are essential. Suppose you want to apply for an entry-level banking position. What qualifications will an applicant need to get that position? Care with details, an aptitude for math, good interpersonal skills, and a customer-service orientation would be likely qualifications. In your application letter, state what you think the need is; then provide evidence for how you meet it.

Example 12.9

Entry-level bankers are asked to perform many mathematical calculations with zero defect. When I was a senior in high school, I was the math expert on our region's academic decathlon team. I received a gold medal for speed and accuracy.

As the banking industry moves away from federal regulation and toward greater competition, I imagine employees with an excellent customer-service orientation will be especially valued. Three summers working in a retail clothing store allowed me to develop my customer-service skills.

III. The call-for-action ending paragraph can be identical to the type used in the job application letter that responds to an advertised position. Remember to keep your tone confident and diffident at the same time.

NONVERBAL ELEMENTS

As with the résumé, controlling the nonverbal messages sent by your job application letter is an important part of your task. Consider the same issues you considered when developing your résumé.

Matching the Résumé

If your application letter and résumé are to be sent together, which is the usual case, use the same paper, the same typeface, and to whatever degree seems reasonable, the same graphic style. Your application will then look like a well-considered package.

If you have chosen a somewhat darker or bolder paper for your résumé—for example, medium gray—you might choose a somewhat lighter coordinating paper for your letter—for example, light gray. Whether you decide to coordinate with or match your résumé, choose the same quality and surface for both papers.

Mailing Etiquette

Multiple pages of a letter are not stapled together. Multiple pages of a résumé are stapled. When your résumé and job application letter are ready to be mailed, place the letter on top of the résumé and fold them together. (This is why the job application letter is sometimes referred to as a cover letter.) If you are using standard business-size envelopes, buy your envelopes to match your letter paper. Almost all good-quality stationery is available with matching envelopes.

When your job application package is received and removed from the envelope, it will bear the marks of the folding. Sometimes it is worth practicing folding your application materials so you can see if the fold makes it difficult to read any of your material. If you find that you do not like the look of your application after it has been folded, you might consider using flat 9 x 12 envelopes. Typically, flat mailers cost a bit more than envelopes and sometimes require additional postage. On the other hand, your application materials arrive as nicely neat and flat as when you prepared them.

The job application letter formally asks that an organization consider your qualifications for a job. The application letter interprets the facts on your résumé. It shows how the skills you possess are applicable to the position you're applying for.

The tools and techniques of the persuasive message strategy are used in modified form in job application letters. The most difficult and important modification is to control the tone of the letter. It must sound confident without sounding self-centered or overbearing. The best way to achieve this tone is to ask assertively for what you want. Don't demand or expect.

As with any persuasive communication, the job application letter focuses on reader benefit—what positive outcomes will occur for the company if it hires you. Incorporate you-attitude and positive phrasing.

Job application letters are the first communication from you the company officers will see. It must be the best writing you can do. Match the nonverbal communication cues of your application letter to the nonverbal cues of your résumé.

An advertised position will provide a list of the qualifications the company would like applicants to have. Use your letter to demonstrate that you have the qualities the company seeks. When you apply for a job that has not been advertised, imagine the qualifications and show how you meet them. In an unsolicited letter, make the beginning more attention getting.

13

The Job Interview

If your résumé and job application letter persuaded the decision makers in an organization, you may be invited for a personal interview. In this chapter, we will address the components of a job interview and identify principles of excellent interviewing.

Interviewing is a communication skill. Like listening, writing, and giving a presentation, interviewing skills can be learned and developed. Preparing for your interview will help you relax and represent yourself in the best light.

THE JOB INTERVIEW

Most people, both those hiring and those being hired, want to talk face-to-face before they make employment decisions. People believe they can tell more about a person by watching him or her communicate. Interestingly, research does not necessarily support this belief. Unless the interviewer is trained in evaluative interviewing techniques, there is no correlation between performance in a job interview and performance on the job.

What most participants in an interview are responding to are first impressions and "chemistry." They respond to stereotypes and associations. Frequently the person conducting the initial employment interview is a recruiter who will never work directly with the applicant, so interpersonal dynamics are relatively unimportant. In spite of these observations, the interview remains a critical hurdle in the path to employment.

The Organization of the Interview

Generally, all interviews use the same organization. Knowing what to anticipate can help you relax and feel in control. Interview organization includes three somewhat distinct phases: the opening segment, the question-and-answer segment, and a closing segment. We'll discuss the major goals of each part individually.

I. The opening phase serves to *establish rapport, provide orientation,* and *motivate the participants* to share information openly.

Usually some "small talk" occurs at the very beginning of an interview. The participants might talk about the weather, a current event of local interest, or a shared hobby—any topic the participants can discuss comfortably without feeling judged. Establishing rapport reduces tension and helps all participants relax.

The opening phase also provides some orientation and direction for the interview. The interviewer can verify some of the basic information like each participant's name and the position being applied for. Applicants often find it helpful to know how long the interview is expected to last.

The third objective of the opening is to establish goals or desired outcomes for the interview. For example, you might find it helpful to know at the very beginning that the company will be making a hiring decision by the end of the week or that the company believes you might fit well in any of three different positions and so wants to find out more about your interests and expectations. Knowing the goals of the interview beforehand can motivate participants to be more open with certain kinds of information.

II. The question-and-answer segment of the interview is its real heart—the reason for the interview. Even though one of the participants is referred to as the interviewer and one as the interviewee, both are expected to ask and answer questions. The employment interview allows the applicant to discuss in greater detail his or her strengths. It also allows the company to sell itself to the applicant. Both sides come prepared with questions they would like to have answers to.

III. The closing segment of an interview begins with a summary of the major points covered. An applicant wants to know when the company will be making decisions, when the applicant can expect to hear, and some sense of whether or not the company is still interested in the applicant.

Group Interviews vs. Individual Interviews

Usually, an interview consists of one representative from the company and one applicant. This situation is the easiest because the interview takes a conversational rhythm. You can answer questions and then listen to the interviewer answer your questions. You can switch smoothly from talking to listening. It is easy to make eye contact. You can identify areas of mutual interest and talk about those. The one-on-one interview is most like the conversational communication you practice daily.

However, more and more organizations are using group interviews. You will feel more comfortable if you are prepared for a group interview as well as an individual interview. In a group interview, you might find two or more company representatives who interview you at the same time, one company representative who interviews two or more applicants at the same time, or even multiple interviewers and multiple applicants. Group interviews result in different types of stresses. The following ideas will help you be prepared.

EXPECT NOISE AND SOME CONFUSION

Several people are bound to start talking at the same time. People get confused about who asked the question and who is to answer the question. Don't let the activity rush you. Take time with your answers. Speak clearly and with enough volume to be heard over background noise.

When you begin talking at the same time as someone else, yield the floor sometimes and continue speaking sometimes, letting the other yield the floor. You will be demonstrating that you have no need to push your way into the limelight. On the other hand, you do not allow yourself to be walked on.

INCLUDE EVERYONE PRESENT

When you are asked a question, begin your response by looking directly at the questioner. Then, as you continue your answer, move your eyes around to include everyone in the room. Use body language to make everyone feel included. Use people's names.

When your answer can build on the answer of someone else, give that person credit. For example, in response to the question "Why would you like to work for our organization?" you might say "Earlier Bill noted that your organization seems to support continued education and training. That's important to me. The organization seems to support its employees in many ways—for example, making sure employees have the tools they need to do their jobs well."

You can even build your questions on the questions of others, again giving them credit. For example, you might respond to the question "Does anyone have any questions?" with "Ms. Blackfoot mentioned your assembly factory just across the border in Mexico. Do you ever assign trainees to work in Mexico?"

Building on what has gone before demonstrates several important qualities. One is that you give credit to others freely and frequently. You also remember people's names and their contributions. You are a team player. Because you pay attention, you don't waste anyone's time.

TAKE AN ACTIVE ROLE

As in the application letter, you are trying to walk a line between confidence and pushiness. If you tend to be shy, you must push yourself to speak up, to take the floor, to talk first sometimes. If you tend to be a talker, you may need to force yourself to let others speak first. You can demonstrate excellent communication skills by remembering that excellent communicators talk and listen well.

Sometimes a group of applicants is asked to solve a problem. Should you find yourself in this position, listen carefully, try to involve everyone, help structure the process. All these behaviors will speak well of your leadership skills.

REMAIN CONFIDENT

After answering a question, you may be asked if you are sure about your answer. Unless you have just remembered additional information that makes your response questionable, stick with your response. You can always acknowledge that there are many solutions for most problems. However, you feel confident the approach you've selected is the most comfortable for you.

Sometimes group interviews make it seem as if your thinking on a particular problem or question is different, out of the norm, and therefore, wrong. Don't be persuaded by peer pressure unless you have truly changed your mind. Sometimes one or more of the candidates in a group interview are actually employees of the company trying to test your integrity and leadership skills.

The Interviewer

Interviewers come in a variety of types. You can remain more relaxed if you think ahead about how you will handle the situation given some of the more common interviewer types.

THE POOR INTERVIEWER

Not all interviewers are trained. Some don't even possess reasonable interpersonal communication skills. In fact, some are downright bad. When you are faced with an interviewer who doesn't seem to be asking you questions that allow you to discuss your qualifications, you will need to take the initiative. In addition to answering questions, you may need to ask them of yourself. For example, you might say, "You may be wondering how I can apply my experience working in a hamburger restaurant to the opening at your company. Actually, there are many similarities in the skills required for both positions."

If the questioner asks very broad, open-ended questions, make them specific as you answer them. For example, you may be asked a question like, "Why did you apply for this position?" As you answer the question, make it increasingly specific. "As you know, accounting is my major. As president of the Accounting Association on campus, I had the opportunity to discuss opportunities at your firm with your Sacramento partner when he came to talk with us on campus. His feedback, combined with information in your annual reports, encouraged me to talk with two of your client companies. They are both impressed with your professionalism and level of customer service."

This sort of interviewer will not make it easy on you. On the other hand, you will be able to demonstrate your ability to adapt to difficult situations, to use your intelligence and creativity, to shine where others who are less prepared will really sound tongue-tied.

THE STRUCTURED INTERVIEWER

Research indicates that one way to improve the predictability of interviews is to structure the interview—to ask the same questions in the same order of each of the candidates. If you find you are being asked a series of somewhat closed-ended questions which seek specific information without allowing you much room for additional explanation, you are being interviewed using a structured format.

In this situation, the way to succeed is to answer the questions directly. Add only the essential detail and evidence. The chances are that the interviewer will ask you about all the relevant information, so just relax and pay attention to the question you are being asked. Listen carefully.

THE STRESS INTERVIEWER

Some interviewers, perhaps because of their own lack of confidence, because of prejudice, or as part of an overall applicant screening process, specifically try to make the interview stressful. These interviewers may attack some of your answers as being "naive" or "stupid." They may question your honesty in response to one or more questions. They may ask you questions which make you uncomfortable—for example, something about your credit history or your sex life. They may keep you waiting or talk on the telephone about what appears to be a somewhat private and sensitive issue.

Should you be faced with such an interviewer, the best response is to make a polite and direct remark. For example, to a rude question, you might say, "Why do you ask?" or "I prefer not to respond to the statement." If the interviewer is on the phone, simply gesture that you will be waiting outside and leave. If you are being kept waiting beyond what seems to you a reasonable time, find the secretary or receptionist and say, "Mr. Zoggo appears to be very busy today. Perhaps we could arrange another interview at a more convenient time."

Be assertive. Look out for yourself. If this is a planned stress interview, being centered and assertive is the way to score well. If this is not a planned situation, your actions may be seen as aggressive and unacceptable. The question then becomes, do you really want to work around people who are this rude anyway?

The Interview Progression

Although people have been hired solely on the basis of their résumés, that is extremely unusual. Somewhat more frequently, an applicant is offered a position about two-thirds of the way through the interview. The most usual hiring process, however, includes a series of two or three interviews.

The first interview is typically conducted by a professional recruiter, perhaps someone from the human resource management department. Universities invite recruiters to come to campus to interview students about to graduate. Larger cities have career fairs where many companies set up booths and talk with interested candidates. Many job candidates apply in person at organizations in their geographical area. Those who meet the qualifications for posted jobs are often interviewed on the spot.

In all these cases, the first interview is a screening interview. Those candidates who show potential are referred to the department which has an open position. Department decision makers then decide on a smaller set of candidates to interview a second time.

The second interview is held at the work site. Frequently it is a group interview with perhaps five to twenty candidates being interviewed on the same day. The on-site interview allows the candidates to become familiar with the organization as the organization becomes more familiar with the candidates. Usually a candidate will speak directly with the person he or she would report to and would get a better idea of the actual working environment. A job offer is usually made at the end of the second interview or within a day or two following.

When organizations hire for upper-level positions, they frequently invite the candidate back for a third interview. Usually the spouse is invited as well, and the company puts itself out to attract the candidate. Realtors take the applicant around the town, an evening party or dinner is held in the applicant's honor, and the spouse may be invited to lunch with other employees' spouses. The candidate will meet with the department in charge of employee benefits.

ON-SITE INTERVIEWING ETIQUETTE

When a candidate is invited to the workplace to interview, the chances are excellent that the interview will last nearly all of a day, perhaps more. That means that applicants will be taken out to eat. When you eat out with representatives of the company, you are still being interviewed and should act as though you are.

Watch what you say, avoid alcohol, do not eat rapidly, do not talk with your mouth full. Order food which is easy to eat—interviewing all afternoon with spaghetti sauce on your front is hard on your sense of confidence. Do not blow your nose at the table, do not comb your hair or apply make-up at the table. For some candidates, these are common sense dictates. For others, they are necessary warnings.

If you are staying over at a hotel, you will also be taken to dinner. The chances are excellent that alcoholic beverages will be ordered by the company representatives taking you to dinner. Be very careful with your own drinking. A day of interviewing is exhausting. When you are tired and under stress, alcohol has much stronger effects. You do not want to undo an entire day's worth of careful processing of information with a second glass of wine.

MINI-BREAKS

In order to reduce the stress of non-stop interviewing, ask for occasional bathroom breaks. Take time to wash your hands and face; comb your hair; take a few deep breaths. No matter how tightly the company has scheduled your time, you have the right (and probably the need) to a few minutes to yourself. Ask for them.

PREPARING FOR THE INTERVIEW

The more you know about the company you have applied to, the position you have applied for, the person or persons who will be interviewing you, and your skills and qualifications, the more prepared, and thus relaxed, you can be. Review Chapter 10 for suggestions on researching jobs and companies.

Anticipate Certain Questions

Researchers, employment agencies, and head hunters all keep data banks on the questions most frequently asked during interviews. Here is a sample of the more common questions.

- What are your professional goals for the next five years?
- What do you know about our company?
- Why do you feel qualified for this position?
- Why should we hire you?
- What were the three things you liked best about your previous job?
- What were the three things you liked least about your previous job?
- What would you say is your greatest strength?
- What would you say is your greatest weakness?

- What do you think your previous boss would say is your greatest weakness?
- Why did you major in _____?
- How did your educational experience prepare you for this job?
- How would you handle a hostile coworker who kept making offensive remarks?
- What experience have you had working under pressure?
- Why did you leave your previous job?
- How would you define an ideal work environment?
- Do you like to work overtime?

Think through possible answers to these questions. Some people, in preparing for interviewing, write out three or four answers for each question. They believe that completely formulating several strong answers for a large number of questions improves their interviewing performance.

POSITIVE PHRASING

Many people want to know just how honest you need to be in your job application process. To some degree, that depends on your personal ethics. In most cases, if you falsely represent yourself, you are subject to immediate dismissal no matter how many years you have successfully performed the job. For instance, an applicant for an assistant professor position in a university English department claimed he had a doctorate from Stanford. He was hired and worked for the university for seventeen years, receiving tenure and promotion. When a variety of circumstances brought his degree into question, and verification indicated the man had never finished his degree, he was fired on the spot.

As a result, for both pragmatic and ethical reasons, you must answer truthfully. You are also allowed to shed the most favorable light possible on your background and qualities.

For example, when asked what you would consider your greatest weakness, make sure you mention the steps you are taking to improve. For example, "I'm pretty impatient. Because I work fast, I expect others to do so as well. I've been working out at the gym regularly, which I find helps me relax and accept that not everyone has my drive." That is much more positively phrased than, "People are always telling me to lighten up and get off their case."

Here's an additional example of positively phrasing the weakness. Rather than, "I procrastinate and miss deadlines," better would be, "My time management skills are weak, so I have signed up for a workshop to be given next month. I have also begun using a daily planner."

ILLEGAL QUESTIONS

Since it is illegal for an organization to make hiring decisions based on race, sex, age, religion, creed, national origin, or handicap, any time an interviewer asks you a question about one of these, the question is probably an illegal one.

What should you do if the interviewer asks if you are Jewish? It depends. You can answer the question. You can say, "Could you tell me why that's a relevant question?" and then address the interviewer's concern. Perhaps the interviewer needs people who are available to work Saturdays. He or she is afraid that if you are Jewish, you won't be willing to work Saturdays. Instead of answering the illegal question, answer the work-related question. Either you can or you can not work Saturdays.

MONEY

Eventually, all potential employees and employers will need to address the topic of money—salary and benefits. However, business etiquette dictates a proper and an improper time to do so. During the first interview, the employer may ask what sort of salary you expect. At that time, it is really not proper to discuss the question. Respond with a statement like, "I'm flexible on salary. I'd rather we waited to discuss that until we've decided I'm the right person for this position."

If providing a salary history was one of the requirements for your application, of course you must do so. You may also note on your salary history that what you've been paid as a waiter working part-time during school is not relevant to your next career-level position.

If you have essentially been offered the position, it is then time to discuss salary and benefits. Do your homework. Make sure you know what people doing this job in your geographical area are paid. When you are asked what sort of salary you are looking for, state your range in a positive and unselfconscious way. In general, organizations expect you to ask for about a 20 percent increase in pay when you change jobs.

NEGOTIATIONS

Do not accept a position on the spot. Ask for two or three days or up to three weeks to consider the offer. Take your time. Weigh all the pros and cons of each offer. Talk to people you trust. Research the salary offer and make sure you are getting a salary similar to others doing your kind of work. If you don't think you are, then ask them to consider increasing their offer. It is now time to be specific about money and benefits. Look at location, opportunity for promotion, training program, benefits, and work characteristics as well as money.

After 25 years of doing business with an Equal Pay Act in force, women in the U.S. continue to receive significantly less than men for equal work. In 1993, women were receiving about 72 cents for each dollar a man received for similar work. Please keep this in mind as you negotiate for your salary and benefits.

Asking the Questioner Questions

All job candidates are expected to want to know a great deal about the company they might work the next thirty years for. As a result, you need to be prepared with questions to ask the interviewer. You can ask your questions throughout the interview, or alternatively, you can wait until the interviewer is done asking you questions. Then you can ask all yours together. In most interviews, the interviewer asks if you have any questions. No matter how informative the interview has been, you are expected to ask questions. They are a way of showing your interest. Here are some of the kinds of questions you might consider asking.

- How long have you worked for this company? What do you think is the best thing about being one of its employees?
- How much responsibility does a person holding this position have?
- What is the typical career path of a person entering the organization at this level?
- What kind of training would I receive?
- How long is it typically before a person entering the organization at this level is promoted?
- Would I be expected to travel?

GOOD NONVERBAL CUES

Interpersonal communication depends a great deal on nonverbal cues to transmit meaning. Typically in an interview, you will want to communicate interest, competence, and enthusiasm. In order to do that nonverbally, try leaning slightly forward. Make frequent eye contact. Keep your shoulders up. Don't slouch in your chair. Do not lean on the interviewer's desk.

The Handshake

In western cultures, the handshake is somehow the measure of a person. A good firm grip indicates warmth and confidence. A weak handshake indicates lack of surety. Extend your arm so your hand makes good contact with the interviewer's hand. Apply pressure to your shake for one to three seconds. During that time, make eye contact, smile, and if possible, say the other person's name. In fact, the handshake is a comfortable time to remind people of your name and ask them to tell you their names.

Women might want to extend their hands first. That settles any awkwardness about who should shake whose hand. Women in business shake hands. Women in employment interviews shake hands—all the time, just like men.

Professional Appearance and Grooming

One of the most important ways we communicate nonverbally is with our dress and grooming. In general in an employment interview, the goal is to look like the interviewer expects you to look. Any time your appearance and grooming do not meet what the interviewer expected, you must overcome additional resistance to hiring you. For example, if you are a male interviewing for a job in banking, the interviewer will not expect you be wearing an earring. If you are wearing one, there will be some degree of resistance to your appearance which you will have to overcome. On the other hand, if you are a male interviewing for a stage manager position for a rock band, wearing one or many earrings would be within the interviewer's frame of expected behavior and so would cause no particular resistance.

DRESS

The general rule for what to wear to an interview is this: Dress for the interview the way you will be expected to dress at work.

If you are applying for a summer forestry job, wearing jeans and a neat and clean shirt would be acceptable and expected, whether you are male or female. On the other hand, if you are applying for a sales representative position at IBM, you will be expected to wear a dark suit and a light shirt or blouse to the interview. If you *really* want a job at IBM, wear a navy blue suit with a white shirt and burgundy tie for men or a light silk blouse and burgundy scarf or jewelry for women. That's the classic look for employees of "Big Blue," and the more you look like one, the more the interviewer will conclude that you will "fit right in."

You can make a mistake in dressing for the interview by being either under-dressed or over-dressed. Here are two stories which prove the point.

A college sophomore was encouraged by his roommate to apply for a summer job as a forest firefighter. He showed up at the appointed time, wearing his interviewing outfit—a nice light grey suit, blue shirt, and navy print tie. He felt the interview went well, however he was not offered the job. He returned to the home of his parents for the summer and worked in a local restaurant.

The next spring, his roommate, who had spent the summer fighting forest fires, again suggested that he apply for the job. He said he didn't want to be turned down again. His roommate laughed gently and said he thought maybe he could help him. It seems his interview had been talked about widely that summer. The interviewer was most amused. He had told everyone, "Those college kids! What did he think we did all summer? Sit at desks and answer telephones!" He had overdressed and in doing so communicated that he didn't understand what firefighters did.

The second story demonstrates the opposite point. The owner of a large sporting goods store was getting ready to open a second store near a university. He advertised clerking positions at the university placement center. He was disappointed and a little angry when students showed up to apply for the positions wearing shorts and thongs. One young male applicant wasn't even wearing a shirt. The owner's response was very similar to the forester's response: "What do they think we do in this store? Lie around in the sun and drink beer!"

The conclusion is find out what the people who do the job you want in the organization you are interviewing with wear, and then wear that. You can complete your research in the parking lot of the company. What are the people who are leaving work wearing? Or you can ask professional acquaintances for their advice. In an absolute pinch, you can call and ask the receptionist for advice. It's better to ask and then wear the expected outfit than to show up over- or under-dressed.

GROOMING

No matter what you end up wearing to the interview, it needs to be clean and neat. And you need to be neat and clean. Make sure your hair is clean and combed.

Men, if you have facial hair, trim it away from your mouth. Clean your nails and polish your shoes. These details are important to others, no matter what level position you are applying for. Looking healthy and conscientious says volumes about the kind of worker you will be.

Women, do not fuss with your hair. If it is long, pin it away from your face. For thousands of years, a woman's hair has been considered a sexual object—that's why many religions require women to cover their hair, especially when they are in church or at a holy service. Since at work you want to convey professionalism, not sexiness, take care not to emphasize your hair. Avoid large jewelry, bracelets which make noise, and earrings with a great deal of movement. All of these detract from your qualifications for the job. In general, dress slightly more conservatively than a man who is applying for the same position. (Is that sexism? Perhaps. Is that practical? Yes.)

TIME COMMUNICATES

One last note about the interview—be on time. Better yet, be early. You can always use the extra time to look at the building and the grounds, to talk with the secretaries, to get something to eat or drink. But being late to the interview communicates nearly everything you don't want communicated. Whether or not you intended it, arriving late to an appointment in the

U.S. communicates lack of interest, a need for attention, and perhaps a need to control others. Not many employers are interested in employees with these traits.

The résumé and job application letter may get you the interview. It is success with the interview that gets you the job. Few employers are willing to hire you unless they like the way you perform in person.

In order to succeed in the interview, prepare in advance. Know everything you can about the company, the position, the interviewer, and your qualifications for the position.

Certain questions come up in a majority of interviews. Consider those questions carefully. Prepare answers before you schedule the interview. You might even ask a friend to help you practice interviewing.

Because so much of face-to-face communication is nonverbal, be aware of what your body, your clothes, and your grooming say about your interest in, and ability to do, the job.

14

Following Up

When you have completed your interview, you are still not finished with the job-hunting process. Whether or not you receive a job offer and whether or not you accept it, you have several more communication situations facing you.

In this chapter, we will address the kinds of communications you will need to complete the job application process. All the letters in this chapter follow message strategies introduced in Chapters 6 and 7.

THE MESSAGE MACHINE

Once you have sent out job application letters, you will of course check the mail anxiously each day. In addition to your address, your resume contains your phone number. Some recruiters prefer the more immediate contact of the telephone over a letter. Prepare to receive phone calls. The best way is to buy or borrow an answering machine to use during your job hunting. Record a simple professional message and check your machine regularly.

(Some answering-machine owners have somewhat creative messages that incorporate music, sound effects, and colorful language. Remember audience analysis and make your message appropriate and professional.)

AFTER THE INTERVIEW

Within a day or two of your interview, you need to take two types of action.

Follow Through on Commitments

First, if you committed to anything during the interview, now is the time to follow through. You might have said you would have an official transcript of your college coursework sent, or perhaps you promised to send information on a topic you discussed in the interview. Potential employers are very impressed when you follow through promptly on commitments you made. You are providing evidence of the sort of worker you will be—one who takes prompt action.

Write Thank-You Letters

Second, write a thank-you letter to everyone who interviewed you. In fact, write a thank-you letter to anyone who helped you with the interview. Perhaps a secretary was especially helpful in getting your plane reservation changed or helping you find your way around a very large office complex. Thank-you letters are quite short—two or three paragraphs. They follow the direct message strategy and are discussed in general in Chapter 6. Here is an outline of the interview follow-up letter.

I. Address the interviewer as he or she introduced himself or herself to you at the interview. If the interviewer used his or her first name, you may do the same in your thank-you letter. On the other hand, if the interviewer used the more formal *last* name, your letter should use that form of address.

II. In the first paragraph, say thank you. Refer directly or indirectly to the position you applied for and the date of your interview. For example, "Thank you for talking with me about the sales trainee position on Wednesday."

Your second sentence can expand your thanks by saying something nice about the interviewer. Match your tone to the level of formality of your interviewer. If the interviewer was an informal type of person, you might say something like "You really helped me relax. I appreciate that." If the interviewer was a more formal person, you can say something like "I appreciated your willingness to answer all my questions."

III. In the middle paragraph, you can take one of two paths. Think of a time when you thought the interview was going particularly well and mention something that will remind the reader of that. For example, suppose after you discussed the internship you had during the summer, the interviewer said how well that experience would support you in this position. In your thank-you letter, you might say something like "I was pleased to hear that you thought my summer internship would allow me to make a contribution to the company right away." If you have been concerned about a weak answer you gave to a particular question, you might want to use your middle paragraph to take a second shot at the question. You can say something like "During the interview, you asked me what I would do if someone I was supervising was hurt on the job. I continue to think about that question. I wish I had said . . ."

IV. As with all direct-message letters, your thank-you letter should end with a forward-looking close. The most obvious is "I look forward to hearing about your decision." You can also personalize the ending. Suppose during the interview the interviewer mentioned that your interest in fly fishing was an interest of his or hers. You might want to end your letter with something like "I look forward to taking you to one of my favorite fishing streams after trout season begins."

This strategy will work just as well for writing to someone who helped you with the interview process, even if he or she didn't interview you. For example, you might want to send a note to those people who said they would serve as references for you. Again, match the level of formality and the tone to the formality of your audience.

Thank-you letters can be typed on stationery or handwritten on cards. Either format is acceptable. If you choose to write your note on a card, many nice cards are available. You can choose one with *Thank you* on the cover or one with any pleasant picture and a blank page inside. In this situation, avoid the card with a prewritten thank-you message inside. The personally written thank-you is significantly better.

Waiting to Hear the Decision

At the end of the interview, the interviewer will probably tell you when you can expect to hear from the company. If that doesn't happen, ask what the next step is. Suppose the day you thought you would hear comes and goes without any word. After five days, you may call or write and ask how the hiring process is coming along and whether the interviewer can give you the current status of your application.

If you are waiting to hear from the company before you make a commitment to another company, you may certainly say so. As with the job application letter, make sure your tone is one of asking or requesting and not demanding or pushing.

IF THE ANSWER IS NO

If the answer is no, you may need to handle some depression or lowered self-esteem. Because you need to keep your confidence up to interview successfully, you may need to find a way to put the rejection in perspective.

The Fit

The most accurate way to think of job hunting is that you are seeking a perfect job-person match. If you don't get the job, that may be all the better. The chances are excellent that the company's representatives know its culture and the job it needs done better than you do. Trust them.

If they've decided not to hire you, they may have saved you from a job they know you wouldn't like or wouldn't handle well. The goal is not to confuse your desire for **a** job with your desire for **this** job. Be grateful. Apply to another company.

Learn from the Experience

If your application for employment is unsuccessful, take the opportunity to learn everything you can from the experience.

KEEP NOTES

Keep a file on every company you apply to. In your file, keep a copy of the job announcement, a copy of all correspondence you sent and received, and notes on the company, the company's culture and employees, the interviewer, and the interview.

You can use your company files for a number of things. First, you will always know the jobs you've applied for. Sometimes when you are getting job announcements from several sources, it's hard to remember to which companies and for which jobs you've applied. Good records answer your questions.

You can also compare the response you get to different versions of your resume or application letter. If you find one version is getting more responses than others, use that version.

Your file of company names and addresses and interviewers' names can be used later for a variety of reasons. If you become a sales representative, perhaps your file can become part of your list of potential customers. Interviewers might make excellent contacts if you want to change jobs in the future.

USE THE FEEDBACK

If you receive any feedback about how you can make your application stronger, try applying it. After the decision has been made, some interviewers are willing to help you by discussing your strengths and weaknesses. Listen carefully. When we've been told we can't have something we want, many of us have a tendency to get defensive. We might focus on proving why the criticisms are false rather than listening for the truth in them. Try to hear what is being said to you.

IF THE ANSWER IS YES

You may hear that you have been offered a job. That message starts another series of steps in the job-hunting process. Your first job is to decide if the company and job still interest you. The interview is a two-way exchange of information, and sometimes applicants discover the fit of person, job, and organization is not good. Perhaps you have received another offer that interests you more. If you decide you do not want to accept the offer, you will need to write a rejection letter.

Telling the Company No

Since the company's representatives have made an offer, you must assume that they will be disappointed if you tell them you are not going to accept the offer. Therefore, the rejection letter uses the indirect message strategy discussed in Chapter 7.

I. Start your letter with a neutral beginning that will buffer the negative news. A rather standard beginning to choose is "Thank you for your generous job offer."

II. Explain your reasons for saying no. If you have accepted another position, you can say so. Here's an example:

Example 14.1

> As I mentioned during my interview, I was also pursuing a position with the XYZ Company. Last week, they offered me the chief accountant's position.

If you feel uncomfortable about the company or the position, you can say so as long as you phrase the discomfort in personal terms. You might say something like the following:

Example 14.2

> I have thought a great deal about the information I learned about the position during our interview. You mentioned that for the first two years, your associates can expect to travel out of town between two and three weeks per month.

III. After you have stated your reasons, phrase your no positively. Attach the negative news to the reasons rather than placing it in a separate paragraph. For example, you need only attach "which I have accepted" to Example 14.1.

To add a no to Example 14.2, you might say something like "I happen to be one of those people who finds it very difficult to sleep away from home. I think my work performance would suffer under those conditions and that I would not be the employee you would expect me to be."

IV. Close on a positive note. The people of this company are already disposed to like you. Retain the good opinion they have of you by saying kind things about them. For example, you might say "Everyone at the company was so nice to me. Every question I had was answered cheerfully, even when I called back for the third time." Another example might be "You have a great team of people working for you. Thank you for asking me to be one of them."

Telling the Company Yes

When employers make you an offer, it's usually because they see an excellent fit between you and the company. The chances are that you will also see the match as a good one, so you will probably be writing a letter of acceptance. An acceptance letter is good news to the receivers, so the direct message strategy is appropriate.

The acceptance letter is also part of a contract, so it must include certain specific information. The letter of offer constitutes the other half of the contract. You are responding directly to the offer letter. Information that must typically be included in your acceptance, specifically or by reference to the offer letter, includes the following:

- starting date of employment
- salary
- job title
- date of acceptance
- your signature

Remember that in the direct message strategy, the acceptance goes in the first sentence. Any explanatory information goes in the middle of the letter. The letter ends with a forward-looking close.

Here's an example of an acceptance letter that uses reference to the offer letter as its starting point.

Example 14.3

I accept your offer of a position as a staff accountant. I understand the terms of the offer and accept them without modification.

I look forward to 8:00 a.m. on July 5. I can't wait to begin my association with you and the rest of the accounting team.

Here's an example where the letter specifies more of the terms. This letter might be written when an offer was made and then you negotiated the starting salary so that it is now different from the amount in the offer letter:

Example 14.4

> I am pleased to accept your offer of employment. I accept all the terms specified in the letter of offer, with the exception of starting salary.
>
> As we agreed on May 7, my starting salary will be $33,000, and overtime will accrue to me only when my weekly billed hours exceed 49 hours per week.
>
> Thank you for working out these changes. I'm so excited, I may not sleep at all between now and next Monday morning. I look forward to being a hardworking member of your team.

In most cases, the company will send you another offer letter when the terms of the offer change, but not always. Just remember that the offer letter and your acceptance constitute your contract of employment. Agree only to what is agreeable. (And good luck with your new job!)

Even after the interview, excellent business communicators have more writing to do. Not all job applicants write thank-you letters, but thank-you letters communicate many positive qualities about the people who do write them. A thank-you letter uses the direct message strategy.

If you receive a job offer and decide you do not want to accept it, you will have to write a letter telling the company so. An indirect message strategy is called for in this situation.

If you want to accept a job offer, your acceptance will constitute your employment contract. Although a thank-you and a rejection could be handled over the phone or face-to-face, the acceptance must always be in writing, dated and signed.

15

Bids and Proposals

So far, the types of business writing we've addressed in this book stress the importance of a conversational tone—creating a personal relationship with the reader of the letter. In this chapter and the next, you will learn about a more formal approach to business communication. The field is generally referred to as technical writing.

Technical writers write bids, proposals, and reports. Rather than developing an interpersonal tone, technical writers distance themselves from their work. They write in the third person, referring to themselves as "the authors" and doing even that infrequently. Their goal is to demonstrate the clarity and logic of their presentation. They want to write so that the facts speak for themselves.

In this chapter, we will discuss bids and proposals, a special subset of technical report writing. In the next chapter, we will discuss the broader category of reports in general.

BIDS AND PROPOSALS

A *proposal* is a presentation, in writing or spoken, that asks that **some idea be considered**. The author of the proposal puts together a logical argument that the idea is a sound one—worthy of attention, money, or time. Some situations where a proposal or bid is commonly used:

- application for grant money
- application to be included in government spending programs

- proposal that one company merge with another
- proposal that one company supply parts or services for another
- proposal that management fund a department's equipment request

Invited Proposals

Certain theories of what constitutes effective and efficient management of organizations are changing. For fifty or more years, economics taught that bigger was better, that by increasing organizational size, companies gained significant economies of scale. When they purchased or produced in large amounts, each individual unit would cost less. Companies integrated vertically and horizontally, taking charge of all the factors in the production of their product or service.

However, today global competition and rapidly changing technology have changed what the marketplace defines as quality. In response, companies must be more flexible. They must be able to change direction rapidly. The very large scale of corporate giants is now hampering efficiency and effectiveness rather than helping it.

Rather than own all the factors of production, an increasing number of companies are choosing to obtain services from people outside the company. When these companies need a service, they send out a Request for Proposals (RFP) or a Call for Bids (CFB) to potentially interested organizations. **Requests for Proposals and Call for Bids invite organizations to submit their ideas or plans for meeting the company's needs**. The RFP or CFB states clearly what the company is looking for, providing technical detail, a deadline date, and usually a desired format for responding.

For example, when the Pacific Gas and Electric Company wants to construct or repair a hydroelectric power plant, they send a CFB to major construction companies asking them to bid on the project. When Nike wants to have tennis shoes made to certain specifications, it seeks proposals from offshore manufacturing companies; it does not own manufacturing facilities in China. When the Department of Defense wants to incorporate quality-management principles, it sends an RFP to management consultants seeking proposals from quality-management training specialists. The RFP or CFB will typically describe an organization's needs and specify the unique requirements that the proposal should cover.

RFPs are used in another situation as well. When a nonprofit foundation such as the Ford Foundation or a government program such as the National Institutes of Health has funds it can distribute to worthy programs or researchers, an RFP will announce the kinds of projects it is interested in funding. People or organizations interested in receiving grants can then respond with a proposal.

Prospecting Proposals

Prospecting proposals are appropriate when an RFP or CFB has not been generated. In a way, **prospecting proposals are like rational sales**

letters, especially in the way they begin. They are essentially descriptions of what the writer or the writer's organization could do if given an award or contract by the reader's organization. In addition to describing what the writer and his or her organization could do, the prospecting proposal needs an attention-getting beginning and somewhat more introductory information that stresses the benefits of the proposal.

Whether invited or prospecting, the goal of a proposal is to present a solution to a problem so convincingly that the proposal is funded. Many companies and all government agencies make most of their orders for supplies and services based on the most desirable proposals. Proposals receive intense attention. Care in preparing them is essential to being granted a contract. In many companies, the proposal is the only sales tool. The company's well being depends on the quality of the proposal.

FORMAT AND ORGANIZATION

Each situation is likely to require a slightly different proposal format. Proposal writers are expected to follow the requirements of the RFP or CFB exactly, so make certain you do. The following are sections typically included in a proposal:

- problem or purpose
- scope of the proposal
- methods or procedures to be used
- materials to be supplied or used
- equipment required
- personnel required
- follow-up
- cost or budget

Proposal writers rarely write the parts of a proposal in the order they appear in the final document. They write them in any order and then assemble the final product, adding transitions where necessary. Although the possible variations are great, consider including the following sections in your proposal.

Problem or Purpose

Most proposals begin with a statement of the problem the proposal will address. The problem should be stated clearly. Usually the writer refers directly to the RFP. The following is an example of the problem section from a proposal to provide the management of an electronics company with information that might reduce its employee turnover:

Example 15.1

Problem Definition

As put forth in your July 10 RFP, ElectroCorp. is interested in reducing employee turnover in the manufacturing section of the Toronto factory. Turnover is costly, and according to company and industry records, ElectroCorp. has for the last two years been experiencing turnover rates significantly higher than average. Hubbard and Associates proposes to address this problem by determining the satisfaction levels of current employees, analyzing exit interview records, evaluating company personnel policies, and comparing ElectroCorp.'s compensation package with that of others in the industry.

A company will probably receive many proposals in response to any request it sends out. Your clear statement of the problem may be the most important part of your proposal. To win a contract or receive funding, you must convince your reader of your clear understanding of the problem.

Some proposals include a section called *Background* that reviews the circumstances leading up to the problem. A background section promotes an understanding of the problem, so is especially helpful in proposals sent to foundations to request funding for a research project.

Each year, about the time the U.S. president sends the budget to Congress, articles appear in the newspapers listing the titles of funded research projects. Taxpayers become agitated when they find $256,000 was awarded to a university professor to study the mating behavior of subterranean termites. Obviously, the professor did a very good job of explaining the background of the problem and why understanding it is important.

Scope

Setting limits on the project is important. Proposal writers must make clear both what they intend to accomplish and what they believe to be beyond the scope of the project. In Example 15.1, above, the proposal writer might want to say that the conclusions will be based on <u>samples</u> of employees from day, night, and swing shifts and that the three groups will be treated separately.

Methods or Procedures

Typically many paths lead to the same destination. In problem solving, many different approaches might be used to reach a satisfactory conclusion. As a result, the methods your company proposes might provide your distinctive advantage—the quality that makes your proposal the best one. Explain the path you intend to take.

Include significant detail. Describe the steps in the sequence in which they will be performed. Include a time line specifying when each step will be completed.

Materials and Equipment

Most proposals list the special materials and equipment required to complete the project. Sometimes an organization's proposal is accepted because it already has the necessary equipment. For example, Harvard's School of Medicine receives many grants for funding medical research. One of the reasons is that Harvard already has a large base of medical material and equipment. The fund-granting foundation will receive more benefit for its dollars because fewer must be spent on developing the baseline equipment.

When materials or equipment must be purchased in order to complete the proposal, the client will be charged for such costs. As a result, specifying the costs clearly is an important part of the proposed contract. Whether the special equipment is already available or must be purchased, discussing required materials and equipment is an important part of the proposal.

Personnel

If the reader of the proposal likes your ideas or methods, he or she will then want to be convinced of your ability to carry through. What often sets one proposal apart from others is the people who will actually perform the work. Discussing the personnel who will be responsible for the project is important.

Most proposals offer brief biographies or résumés of the principal participants. They might also indicate similar work the organization has done for other clients.

Follow-up

When an organization hires an outside firm to complete a project, one of the major concerns is follow-up. What if the job is not done well? What if the problem is not truly solved? As part of convincing the reader to accept your proposal, consider specifically addressing the issue of follow-up. Do you warranty your work? Will you come back in six months and check to see that your system is still working? Is a technical assistant available if questions arise?

When you address issues of follow-up directly, you reduce resistance to your proposal. As Sam Walton, founder of Wal-Mart, said, "Underpromise and overdeliver." Don't suggest that your methods will do more than you know they can do.

Budget

As with any selling-buying relationship, eventually price must be addressed in the proposal. You may simply state a flat fee for providing the product or service addressed in your methods section. More common, however, is including an entire budget in the proposal. When the funding will be disbursed slowly, the proposal writer might even include a cash flow statement.

DESIGN AND PRESENTATION

Your proposal will communicate a great deal about the overall quality of your work and your attention to detail. Your goal is to make your proposal an excellent representative of your work. Of course, you will want to follow required guidelines exactly. And spelling, grammar, and proofreading will be expected to be perfect. However, that's only the beginning.

The standards for design and presentation of proposals are very high. You must use high-quality stationery, clear professional type, and an appropriate cover. The cover will keep your pages clean and in order. Remember to make your left margin larger when you are binding pages.

Consider the overall look of your page layout. You might consider including a border or a touch of color to each page. Perhaps a two-column format would give your proposal a distinctive look. Without letting the design overpower the message, work to make your proposal look special and professional. In general, you want the presentation of your proposal to say nonverbally that you have all the skills necessary to do an excellent job.

One final note about the presentation of proposals: if you are given a deadline, make sure your proposal arrives slightly early. Once again, you can use nonverbal cues to indicate you understand what it takes to do the job well. You not only pay attention to detail; you also get your work done in a timely way.

Proposal writing will be increasingly important to business writers in the next decade. Proposals serve as contracts between funding organizations and organizations or people who will provide a service.

Proposals also serve as marketing tools. Companies or individuals typically compete to have their idea accepted. As a result, all proposals include an element of persuasion. Some portion of that persuasion is the result of having an excellent idea and an excellent plan for following through on the idea. An additional portion arises from attention to details. Such attention indicates nonverbally that the writer is competent and able to complete the task at a quality level.

A forceful argument and logical presentation supersede a friendly tone in importance. Unlike letter- and memo-writing situations, developing a personal relationship with the reader is not part of the goal. Proposal writers distance themselves grammatically from what they are writing, letting the ideas stand alone.

16

The Formal Report

*T*he term *report* is used to refer to a wide range of communication formats. A report can be as short as a memo or as long as multiple volumes. It can be stored on computer disk, presented orally, or printed at typeset quality. In general, however, the term *formal report* refers to a written factual documentation of some aspect of the business.

You will do a better job of preparing reports if you think of them as providing answers to business questions. Some report writers get so entangled in preparing the report they forget their job is not to write reports but to provide answers to questions in an organized and useful way.

The following are the most common purposes of reports:

- to monitor and control operations
- to implement policies and procedures
- to comply with regulatory agencies
- to obtain business funding
- to document work for clients
- to guide decisions

REPORT-WRITING STRATEGIES

How much you will use reports will depend on the company you work for and the job you do. The odds are that you will use reports frequently. The bigger the company or the more complex and technical the work, the greater the odds.

The same principles of message strategy and clear writing apply to writing reports. If you believe the decision makers in your audience will want to hear your conclusion, begin directly. State the conclusion first. On the other hand, if you need to overcome resistance to your conclusion, consider using the indirect approach. Lead up to your conclusions by presenting your reasons and benefits first. Your organization process will go much more smoothly if you specifically address the following questions <u>before</u> you begin preparing your report.

Who initiated the report? If you volunteered to investigate a business problem, you will need to provide your reader more background information. On the other hand, if you were assigned the topic, the person requesting the information will already know the topic was worth pursuing.

What is the business question to be answered by your report? Rather than thinking about your report as documentation of work you've done, think about it as the conclusions you've reached on an important business question. Identifying the question your report is to answer before you begin will help with your research, your documentation, your organization, and your writing.

Is this report routine or special? Many reports are routine, prepared regularly. Examples are monthly expense reports, weekly sales reports, annual profit-loss reports. When a report is routine, questions of organization have already been answered. Use the format typically used for this sort of report. On the other hand, when a report is special, you will need to include information on why the report is necessary. You will need to identify specifically the business question being answered.

Is this report for internal or external users? If your report is five or fewer pages and your readers are in your company, most report writers recommend you use the memo format. Type the report as though it were a memo to the decision maker or the person who asked the question. When your report is for an external user—for example, an advertising campaign for a client or the company's annual report— your report will probably take the form of a typed manuscript.

Some additional points need to be considered as well. Although many reports are no longer than a long business letter, many are very long and contain very complex information. As a result, you will need to

- present the information in a clear order
- show the relationships of various parts of the report
- use visual aids
- use headings and subheadings

The more complex your information, the more helpful outlines will be. Outline your report before you begin writing. This advice is especially important if you are writing the report with a group of people. It will help everyone stay organized and enable the various parts of the report to be integrated easily.

PARTS OF A FORMAL REPORT

The most formal reports contain all of the following parts, in the order listed:

Prefatory parts:

1. title fly
2. title page
3. letter of authorization
4. letter of transmittal, preface, or foreword
5. synopsis, executive summary, or abstract
6. table of contents and table of illustrations

The report proper:

1. introduction
2. report findings
3. conclusions, recommendations, or summaries

Appended parts:

1. bibliography
2. appendix
3. index

Because this discussion of report writing touches only lightly on most of these, be sure to consult examples of reports prepared by others in your organization and look for more information in books about technical writing. Most textbooks, on any subject, can serve as examples of what a formal report looks like. They usually contain all the parts and incorporate good examples of clear organization, headings and subheadings, transitions, introductions, and summaries. Most textbooks are the equivalent of a formal report.

As a report becomes less and less formal, more of the parts are omitted. For example, only the most formal of reports has a title fly, and only longer reports require indexes. A report with no tables or illustrations would obviously not have a table of illustrations.

Title Fly

This page includes the report title. That's all. Usually the title is centered and about one-fourth of the way down the page.

Title Page

The title page includes the report title, the author, the author's company and so on, and the name of the person who authorized or will receive the report. Frequently the date is also included.

When constructing a good title, try to answer the questions *who, what, where, when,* and *why.* Titles should always answer questions, not ask them. For example, the title "Should ECG Company Build a New Factory?" would be more effective if changed to "ECG Expansion Recommendations—1993–1998."

Letter of Authorization

The objective of a letter of authorization is to authorize the investigator to begin the investigation. In the construction industry, for example, a client will request a contractor to prepare a bid for a project. A copy of the client's request letter is included in the report.

Should you be required to prepare a letter of authorization, follow the direct message strategy, including authorization, a clear statement of objective, any limitations (such as time and cost), and special instructions. Usually the client will be charged for the costs associated with preparing a report. As a result, the letter of authorization establishes the contract between the company or person requesting the report and the company or person preparing the report. Correctness is essential.

Letter of Transmittal, Foreword, or Preface

Most formal reports contain some form of personal communication from the writer to the reader. In a textbook, this takes the form of a preface. In any text, the author's name appears at the end of the preface, just as it would at the end of a letter. The style of the preface is more personal than the rest of the book. Generally, the author welcomes the reader and explains how the book should be used.

In a formal company report, this message is prepared exactly like a letter, complete with return address and so on. The letter should follow the direct message strategy, beginning with a statement like "Here's the report you requested on . . . " Following this statement of transmittal or transfer comes a brief identification of the subject matter and possibly a short summary. If any problems arose during the preparation of the report, they are sometimes addressed in the letter. Here's an example: "Although we had originally intended to do primary research, so much secondary research data were available, we relied on them." Frequently, the letter also includes thank-yous and acknowledgments. (Sometimes in books, these acknowledgments are in a separate part.)

Synopsis, Executive Summary, or Abstract

A synopsis is the report in miniature. It concisely summarizes the essential content of the report. It is designed primarily for the busy executive who may not have time to read the whole report. Usually a synopsis is

5–15 percent of the length of the report. (See the section "Preparing an Executive Summary" which appears later in this chapter.)

Table of Contents and Table of Illustrations

Even very short reports can benefit from a table of contents. Essentially, a table of contents is the outline for the report, with page numbers. The headings used in the table of contents should be exactly the headings of the report—that is, they should be phrased the same and be indented to indicate relative importance. Once again, any textbook will serve as an excellent example. If the report includes many illustrations or tables, a separate table of tables or table of illustrations may be helpful to the reader.

The Report Proper

Audience analysis and clear statements of objective are essential in properly organizing the report. As with any other communication problem, the best way to organize the report is a function of the audience's expectations and most likely response to your material. Use whatever strategy you believe is appropriate, given your objective and your audience. If your report is longer than a page or two, use headings to help the reader locate specific information quickly.

Bibliography

Always give credit to others for their work. It's good business, it's good writing, and it's the law. To avoid copyright violations, you must carefully acknowledge the work of others. In some cases, each section of a long report has its own bibliography. In any case, a complete bibliography follows the text of the report.

There are several standard formats for referencing bibliographic material. Check with your company to see which method is preferred, and then follow it exactly and consistently. No matter which format you use, you need to include the following information when your source was documented in print:

- author's name—last, then first—spelled correctly
- title of the article
- title of the book, journal, or newspaper
- publication date
- publication city
- page numbers for the information you used

If your information came from an interview rather than a printed source, you will need the following information:

- interviewee's name, both first and last, spelled correctly
- date
- place

Appendixes

Sometimes including all the detail in the body of your report will make it cumbersome and awkward to read (and write). In those cases, attach the information to the end of your report (and tell your reader you have done so at the logical place in the report.) For example, if your report discusses the findings of a questionnaire of customers, you might want to include a copy of the questionnaire in an appendix. Each type of information should have its own appendix. For example, you might have "Appendix A—Questionnaires" where you include the three different questionnaires you used to obtain the data in your report; "Appendix B—Questionnaire Data" where you include tables of all the data you collected; and "Appendix C—Glossary" where you provide a dictionary of terms your reader may not be familiar with.

Index

An index is an alphabetical guide to the subject matter of a piece of writing, complete with the page numbers where each subject appears. It helps the reader find specific topics. Modern word-processing equipment makes the preparation of an index relatively easy, so more and more reports are likely to contain an index. Once again, any text will provide an example of an index.

PREPARING AN EXECUTIVE SUMMARY

Most reports, especially long ones, are read by many readers reading for different purposes. The person who is responsible for taking action on the report's recommendations is likely to read the entire report very carefully. As the report is passed upward through an organization, the readers are less and less likely to read the entire report. The marketing people will want to pay special attention to those recommendations that specifically affect them. Production readers will be more interested in the changes they will be expected to make. Top management may want to read only enough to get an overview. Therefore, an efficient and effective summary of the report is essential. And because it will become the most widely read part of the report, paying special attention to its preparation is well worth the time.

An informative summary or abstract states the report's problem and scope, describes its method of investigation, enumerates results and conclusions, and lists recommendations.

The following guidelines will help you to draft a consistent, logical summary-abstract.

1. Find out how long the summary should be. If that information is not available as a standard in your company, assume the summary should be about 10 percent of the report's length.

2. Read the report (or article) once for overall comprehension; reread the report; and make note of the overall thesis.

3. Read the report again and highlight every unique term, procedure, or method that should be noted.

4. Examine the report for sections or memorable words you think the abstract should quote verbatim.

5. Compose a short outline with the thesis at the top and the main ideas of the report ranked either by importance or order of appearance in the report.

6. Draft the summary and proceed with the usual review process until the document is polished.

Much of your success in writing a good summary will be determined by your skill in directness and word economy. But in your efforts to be concise, you are likely to end up with a dull writing style. Given the importance of your task, work hard to give your summary a touch of color and style as well as economy of space.

USING VISUAL AIDS

Many people are highly visual. They depend on images, pictures, graphs, or maps to help them understand what they are reading. Using visual aids in your reports will greatly improve your communication with visually sensitive readers.

An amazing array of computer-assisted tools is available for developing visual images. Graphics programs, clip-art programs, and optical scanners make it easy to develop and incorporate visual aids in your reports. These particular tools are relatively inexpensive, and they make a very big impact.

Principles of Graphic Design

Even if you aren't a graphic artist, using some principles of graphic design will result in your visual aids supporting your ideas rather than conflicting with them. Visual aids communicate symbolically. We believe, on a symbolic level, that a dark thick line implies more power than a pale thin one. We associate straight lines with power and strength—curved lines with flexibility and receptivity. Long lines imply permanence and long-term thinking; short lines indicate mortality and short-term ideas. Dark, bold colors are seen as powerful and strong. Pale, pastel colors are associated with creativity and play. Some other principles of graphic design include the following.

THE PRINCIPLE OF CONTRAST

When you want to indicate visually that two ideas or alternatives are very different or in sharp contrast with one another, use strongly contrasting colors to represent them. For example, you might use black and white or red and blue. On the other hand, you can indicate visually that two ideas are related by representing them visually with related colors or with softer, more pastel colors. For example, you might represent two similar alternatives both with blue, using blue dots for one and blue hatchmarks for the other. That idea would be especially good if you wanted to show that two alternatives were quite similar and that both were quite dissimilar from a third choice which you could represent with red.

Any discussion of color in visual aids needs to address the topic of color blindness. About one-tenth of all men suffer some degree of color blindness. The most common form is red-green color separation problems. For people with color-separation difficulty, the two colors appear similar. As a result, never use red and green together. Since in many cultures, green is a color with negative connotations, you are probably best to avoid green rather than red in visual aids.

THE PRINCIPLE OF CONTINUITY

Once you choose a particular format for your visual aids, your audience will expect you to follow that format consistently. For example, if you have listed a series of products and their return on investment on Table 1, and you are listing the same series of products and their cost per ton on Table 2, your audience will expect the products to be listed in the same order. If you have represented your favorite alternative as yellow in Chart 1, the audience will assume that in Chart 2, yellow represents your favorite alternative again.

Think of your visual aids as a related series and apply the graphic design principle of continuity to them.

THE PRINCIPLE OF EMPHASIS

In general, we believe whatever receives the most attention is the most important. Because strong lines, strong colors, and bold geometric shapes give emphasis to points, make certain you are using them on the points you wish to emphasize. If you are develping a pie chart to show the contribution your product makes to the total company profits, color your slice red and color the other slices lighter colors like pink, lavendar, and light blue.

If you are preparing a bar chart in gray scale (all the colors from black to white), make the bar you wish to emphasize solid black and make the other bars shades of gray or use hatchmarks for them. Visually emphasize the points you want the reader to see as most important.

*R*eport writing offers one of the largest communication challenges to business commmunicators. Because reports require a clear and logical analysis of information, they must be well thought out, well researched, and well presented.

Because they tend to be longer than other types of business writing, reports demand clear organization. Report writers must think carefully about their audience, their purpose, and their information. They will want to use headings, transitions, visual aids, and summaries to help their readers identify the main and supporting points of the report.

Thinking of the report as the answer to a business question will help keep report-writers on track. Many report-writers get so involved in the massive task of collecting and analyzing data, they forget their purpose. Reports should answer questions, not serve as a vehicle for demonstrating the amount of work the report-writer went to getting ready to write the report.

17

Nonverbal Communication

In this last section of the book, we will address topics that have to do with interpersonal communication—with communicating face to face. A significant portion of face-to-face communication occurs as the result of interpreting what the face and body of the other person are saying. Some researchers believe that as much as 93 percent of the meaning in a face-to-face interaction comes from the nonverbal cues and symbols.

Much of the meaning we make of nonverbal cues is subconscious. More than any other part of communication, the context in which a behavior is observed influences what the behavior means. A dictionary of nonverbal cues does not exist. As a result, the excellent communicator must take many factors into consideration all at once when determining what meaning to make of nonverbal behavior.

Most people have a more difficult time controlling what their bodies and faces say than what their mouths say. As a result, we tend to trust the nonverbal messages more than the verbal messages. This chapter provides an introduction to what is known about nonverbal communication.

NONVERBAL COMMUNICATION

Whenever you communicate, there are three parts to your message: the words, the sounds, and the movements of your face and body. The words are defined as verbal communication. In the first four parts of this book, we emphasized the importance of word choice and word order in communicating the intended message. In this chapter, the focus will be on the remainder of the message, the nonverbal elements.

Cultural Influences

The most important observation about nonverbal communication is that it is largely **culturally specific.** With very few exceptions, there is no such thing as universally understood nonverbal cues. Some researchers claim that laughing, frowning, and crying are fairly universal in their meaning. However, accurate interpretation of nonverbal messages is culturally dependent. For example, someone in the U.S. is most likely to communicate embarrassment by lowering the head or blushing. In Japan, embarrassment is shown by laughter and giggling. In Saudi Arabia, embarrassment is indicated by sticking the tongue out slightly.

Learning a foreign language is easy compared to learning a foreign culture, and knowledge of the culture is critical to understanding much of the nonverbal portion of a message. Unless otherwise noted, the information in this chapter relates to nonverbal messages delivered within the context of the United States' culture.

Verbal/Nonverbal Consistency

Communication occurs as a result of three different symbol codes: words, sounds, and body posture. Sometimes these three codes are not synchronous. The words can say one thing, the voice tone can indicate another, and the body cues can convey yet another message. For example, someone might walk into a room, slamming the door, taking a deep sigh, and saying "How is everyone this beautiful day?" Trying to decode the symbols and make meaning of them will be difficult. The message will be mixed.

When a discrepancy exists among the three different message systems, research shows communicators tend to believe the nonverbal message is the accurate one. When voice quality and body language are in conflict, body language is usually interpreted as the more accurate coding system. As a result, effective communicators try to **match their verbal and nonverbal messages** so they reinforce one another.

Pervasiveness of Communication

One last general point about nonverbal communication is it is **impossible not to communicate.** Even when a person has no particular meaning in mind, observers will conclude meaning. For example, imagine that you usually stop at the grocery store on your way home from work. Should people draw some conclusion about you by the way you are dressed in the grocery store? Whether they should or not, they do. Whether you intend to send messages or not, at all times others who observe you reach conclusions about you. The effective communicator keeps this observation in mind. If others seem to be drawing conclusions about your meaning which you do not intend, think back over your nonverbal messages. Perhaps you communicated unintentionally.

A great deal of communication occurs as the result of **voiced non-words**—things like sighs, squeals, exclamations, uh, and um. These voiced nonwords add emotion to the meaning which results from the words.

Paralanguage is relatively easy to control. Voice teachers can help speakers reduce their voiced nonwords and modulate their volume, rate, and pitch. Many would-be actors have taken voice lessons to help them change the quality of their voices. However, even with a speaker who has had voice training, someone who is used to the normal voice quality of that speaker will be able to tell when there is tension or joy in the speaker's voice.

Body Language

Body language refers to the movements of the eyes, face, and body of a speaker. It includes not only what a speaker does with his or her arms, for instance, but also how closely the speaker stands or sits to others. It includes what the speaker wears, how as well as where the speaker sits in relationship to others. It even includes when a person arrives for a meeting. All of these topics will be addressed in this chapter.

MAJOR USES OF NONVERBAL COMMUNICATION

Certain kinds of meaning are more apt to be communicated nonverbally than verbally. These include status, power, liking, group membership, and conversation flow.

Interest and Liking

Eye contact can be used to indicate your interest in someone. Holding your gaze signals that you are interested in the person you are talking with or in the subject being talked about. In business, most people expect those they are talking with to look at them. Researchers have found that a person will like you more if you hold eye contact longer and make eye contact more frequently.

Another way you can communicate your interest nonverbally is to stand closer to the people you are speaking with. In the U.S., speakers normally stand 1 1/2–4 feet apart. Standing closer than that indicates intimacy. Standing further apart than that indicates a more formal or more distanced relationship. This cultural norm is so expected that when two people say something to one another at closer than six inches, all observers will jump to the conclusion that "something is going on."

When a person's sense of personal space is invaded, he or she will move to make the interpersonal distance comfortable. If you find yourself constantly backing away from someone, it is a cue to you that you do not feel comfortable having that person "close to you." If others back away from you, "give them some breathing room." (Notice how much of our feeling or emotional language is tied to our nonverbal movements.)

Once again, it is important to note that the normal social distance between people depends on their culture. In France, business colleagues stand much closer to each other than in the U.S. (one to two feet.) In Japan, business colleagues stand much further apart (about four feet.)

Conversational Flow

Given how frequently interpersonal communicators switch from the role of speaker to the role of listener, it is amazing how well we use nonverbal cues to control the flow of conversation. Without thinking, the speaker sends signals when he or she is about to quit talking and let the other speak. Here are some of the signals which control conversational flow.

In general, the speaker does not make eye contact, the listener does. When a speaker is about ready to yield the floor, he or she will begin making eye contact. When the speaker would like the conversation to end rather than to have the listener talk, he or she might stop talking but not make eye contact. In that way, additional permission to speak has not been granted and the message is the conversation is over.

Speakers also indicate they are nearly finished talking by rounding down their voice tone. They slow the speaking rate and drop the pitch. That indicates a willingness to yield the floor.

A third way in which speakers use nonverbals to control the flow of conversation is with their hands. If you, as a speaker, want to "hold the floor" and retain the right to speak, keep your hands above your waist. As you are ready to quit talking, allow your hands to drop down below your waist. If you happen to be one of those people who feels constantly interrupted, check your nonverbals. Perhaps you are signaling to others that it is their turn to talk without realizing you are doing it. When you really want to retain control of a conversation, hold your hand up in the classic traffic police "stop" sign. You will find you have effectively stopped interruptions.

Group Membership

When a person wants to join a group, he or she will nonverbally indicate that desire. If the group is willing to incorporate a new member, they will say so. On the other hand, if the group is unwilling to assume a new member, the members will not respond to the nonverbal request. Handling this issue nonverbally allows everyone to save face.

What are the nonverbal behaviors which indicate the desire to join? One is eye contact. The person desiring to be incorporated into the group makes eye contact with one or more members of the group. Another is physical distance. The outsider approaches the group but remains slightly outside it. If the group is willing to accept the outsider, they will move to "make room for one more."

Status

In the U.S., we have a stated cultural value that all people are created equal and have the same rights. We claim to have a society free of classes. In practice, we have very specific ways to communicate differential status nonverbally.

SPACE

We communicate status by sharing certain cultural norms about space. These norms include the following.

The more space, the better. A large office is better than a small one. A large car is better than a small one.

The more privacy, the better. A private swimming pool is better than the municipal pool. A private golf course is better than the city golf course.

The higher, the better. The most expensive apartments are always on the top floor of an apartment building. The best homes are built highest on the hill.

The more windows, the better. Actually, this has more to do with view than glass. An office with three windows is better than one with no window.

The more expensive, the better. The more expensive the boat, the better. The more expensive the wine, the better.

The more attractive, the better. Many studies demonstrate that workers perform better in prettier surroundings. Other studies have found that people who are perceived as attractive are granted more status and privilege.

Corporations apply these culturally accepted norms to create very clear messages of status and its resultant power. The President of the firm will have large offices on the top floor with windows and views in more than one direction. The janitors will have small tool store rooms with no windows in the basement of the building. The President will have a personal parking space. The janitors will park wherever they can find spaces.

TIME

As a culture, we also share certain beliefs about time. They include the following.

Time is limited. Time is a scarce commodity. You have only so many hours in a day.

Time is linear. We are born, we grow, then we die. There is a past, a present, and a future.

Because we believe these to be true about time, we believe that "how you spend it" is a large indicator of what you think is important. One way you can indicate you really like someone is to "spend" time with them. When a relationship is losing its importance, you might find you are too busy to spend time together.

We use time to communicate status and power. The person of lower status waits for the person of higher status. For example, medical doctors are perceived as having high status in this country. As a result, the patient may expect to spend significant time waiting for the doctor.

If your boss asks you to meet her for lunch at Mackay's at noon, you will get there no later than 11:55 am. The lower status employee waits for the higher status employee.

THINGS

We communicate our status and our interests by the things we have. A manager is identified by his or her briefcase, suit, and Cross pen. A staff person is identified by the brown bag, sweater, and Bic pen. A construction worker is identified by his or her metal lunch pail, hard hat, and mechanical pencil. An interesting observation about things, especially about clothes is that what you think of your clothes and appearance isn't nearly as important as what others think of them. You can argue with the saying, "clothes make the person," but if others believe it, your potential will be judged by it. Many companies have dress codes because they have evidence that clothing has a significant impact on a company's image and sales.

Many experts on recruiting and hiring employees say that you never get promoted to a position you don't look like you belong in. In other words, dress like those who hold the job you would like to be promoted into. If you dress like a secretary, it will be difficult for your boss to see that you would be the ideal candidate for the supervisor's position.

Other things can communicate as well. Interestingly, the shape of things is frequently a powerful nonverbal communication cue. For example, round tables encourage equality. People gathered around a round table feel more free to contribute to the group. England's mythical King Arthur sought to develop a consultative government. He wanted his knights to assist him in the governing of the country. It is no accident that his knights sat around a round table.

Sitting across a table from the person you are communicating with leads to more power struggles. When labor and management meet to discuss labor issues, they frequently "sit across the bargaining table." When groups meet across the table, it is hard for them to see themselves as being "on the same side," on the same team.

INTERNATIONAL BUSINESS COMMUNICATION

Since nonverbal cues communicate so powerfully, and since nearly all nonverbal cues are meaningful only in a cultural context, communicating interpersonally in the international company is critically important *and* exceedingly difficult. Patience on everyone's part will help. Researching the major cultural differences will help. Relying more on written documentation will help.

You are communicating all the time, intentionally or unintentionally. You can choose not to say anything with words, but your body speaks loudly anyway. The effective communicator realizes the power and pervasiveness of nonverbal communication and works to get the verbal and nonverbal messages in harmony—in support of one another.

Accurate interpretation of nonverbal cues depends on an understanding of the culture within which the cue was used. If you are supervising or being supervised by someone of a different subculture, check out your assumptions before acting on them. And if you are communicating internationally, learn what you can about the nonverbal language of your host country.

Nonverbal cues are effective at indicating interest and liking, group membership, and status and power. Nonverbal cues also keep conversation flowing smoothing.

18

Listening

To be an excellent communicator, you need to master the skills of reading and writing, speaking and listening. So far, this book has devoted most of its attention to the skill of writing as it is practiced in business. We have assumed that you have competent reading skills. In this chapter, we will discuss listening and address how you might improve your listening skills. In the next chapter, we will work on speaking skills.

It is accurate to refer to listening as a skill. Like writing, listening can be improved by applying certain principles or approaches. And as is the case with writing, listening improves with practice. This chapter will introduce you to the skills of listening and offer you the opportunity to practice your skills.

THE NEED TO DEVELOP LISTENING SKILLS

In the 1970s, the Sperry Corporation hired several consultants to help them improve their overall delivery of quality product. The consultants observed that the typical employee could remember no more than twenty percent of what he or she had been told only 24 hours earlier. Indeed, when questioned about material they had just heard, the employees were likely to get facts mixed up.

The management of Sperry decided that improving the listening skills of its customer service representatives could greatly increase the company's responsiveness to customer needs. They brought in a team of trainers to develop customer service representatives' listening skills. They were so overwhelmed with the difference improved listening skills made in that department, they expanded the training throughout the firm. Today, all Sperry employees attend training workshops to develop their listening skills and they are required to attend refresher courses periodically. In fact, Sperry Corporation has become such a devoted practitioner of improving listening skills that they now offer listening skill development workshops to other organizations.

Sperry's experience serves to highlight several observations about listening skills. The first is that, in general, our listening skills are not very good. Throughout your schooling, you have practiced reading and writing and talking. Most people have never had a course in listening.

The second is that listening is like any other skill—we are not born knowing how to do it well, but we can learn. Third, applying specific principles and practicing them are effective methods for improving listening.

Peters and Wasserman, in their book *In Search of Excellence*, identified the ability to listen, especially to customers, as one of the keys to corporate success. Edward Deming's work on quality control reinforces this point. He says that at each level of an organization, employees have "customers" or users of their services. In order to provide quality support, all employees at all levels need to listen to their customers.

BARRIERS TO EFFECTIVE LISTENING

Whenever people are not doing something well which could make a difference in their lives, there is a reason for it. Several barriers get in the way of effective listening. Identifying those barriers might help you overcome them and speed your way toward improved listening.

Processing Speed

The ears can take in sound and the brain can process information much more rapidly than speakers speak. The result is that listeners have a great deal of available brain time while they are listening to someone. Without training, most listeners use the time to think of things other than what is being said to them. They think about what they will say next, they judge what the speaker is wearing, they daydream, they plan what they will have for dinner. With practice, you can put your brain to work to help you listen better. You can identify the speaker's main points, relate those points to ideas you've had, work to avoid reaching conclusions before the speaker is finished, and perhaps take notes.

Physical Barriers

If a lawn mower is running right outside your office window, hearing your subordinate's message will be made more difficult. Whenever the environment interferes with the physical capacity to hear, listening will be significantly less effective. Many workers, working in noisy environments, wear earplugs. If you do not realize that, you might say something and get no response. The earplugs are a physical barrier. External noise, physical distance, and physical barriers may all contribute to poor listening.

Psychological Barriers

Each person in an interpersonal communication brings his or her own set of emotional concerns and experiences. If you received a low grade on your chemistry exam, it is very difficult to forget about that and pay attention in your finance class. If you are concerned about meeting an important deadline, it is hard to give your attention to a subordinate who is experiencing computer phobia. If you are thinking about a very special date, you are likely to pay little attention to the presentation being given by the marketing director. Your psychological state can either support or interfere with your ability to listen well.

Each person in an interpersonal communication also brings his or her own set of biases or prejudices. It is likely that you have a bias against listening carefully to someone from one of the following groups.

- A colleague of the opposite sex
- A coworker from an ethnic group other than your own
- Someone much older or much younger than you
- A coworker with whom you feel competitive
- Someone whose mannerisms or personal appearance displeases you
- A coworker whom you judge to be less competent than you

Acknowledging emotional and attitudinal biases allows you to compensate for them and minimize their effects.

Physiological Barriers

Veterans of World War II frequently suffer severe hearing loss. The battlefield was so noisy that the soldiers' ears were permanently damaged. Research shows that people, especially young people, who use stereo earphones have a high danger of permanently harming their ears for much the same reason. Listening to sound above 85 decibels for longer than two hours at a time causes permanent hearing loss. Excessively high sound levels can cause permanent hearing loss in much less time. The Occupational Safety and Health Administration sets noise standards for all employees. Employees working in high-noise environments must be provided with ear protection devices.

The body's ability to *focus* on the task of listening may also be impaired. When you are very hungry, it is hard to think about anything other than food. When you don't feel well, your listening skills will not be as good. Illness, fatigue, worry, and discomfort will make it difficult for you to concentrate.

All of these barriers arise normally in human interaction. You can't make them go away. However, by acknowledging them, you can work around them. If you tend to have low energy about five in the afternoon, plan to have your most important meetings earlier in the day. If you have trouble hearing over the noise in the hallway, close your door. If you are distracted by worry or illness, suggest another time for meeting with someone who needs your attention.

STAGES IN THE ART OF LISTENING

Listening is a complex art. You can listen at different levels of attentiveness. Each of the levels will be appropriate for different situations. The difference between an effective and an ineffective listener is that the ineffective listener rarely advances beyond the first two stages. Each successive level of listening requires a greater commitment and a greater expenditure of energy.

Hearing

The most simple stage of listening is hearing. **Hearing is the physical process** of receiving and decoding the sounds. Sometimes even the hearing stage is difficult to achieve. As was mentioned earlier, twenty million Americans are hearing impaired. They have difficulty receiving the physical signals of sound.

Sometimes external noise gets in the way of hearing. If you work on the shop floor or around equipment or at an airport, the environmental noises will make it difficult to hear voices and especially difficult to hear voice tone and quality. Significant miscommunication occurs at the hearing stage of listening. You might think of hearing as the "uh huh" level of listening—if the listener says, "uh huh" each time the speaker pauses, only the most shallow form of listening is occurring.

IMPROVING HEARING

To improve listening at the level of hearing, take charge of your environment. Shut the window, close your door, leave the shop floor; remove your conversation from the source of physical distractions. It is amazing the number of people who try to yell over noise rather than moving away from the noise source. When the "background" music in a restaurant is so loud that you can't hear the foreground conversation, ask that the music be turned down, or ask for another table further from the stereo speakers. You need not be a victim of the environment. Your communication with others is too important.

Attending

The second level of listening is called *attending* because it involves **paying attention**. A listener who is paying attention is more involved in the listening process. You will usually be able to tell when the people you are speaking to are (1) not hearing you, (2) hearing you but responding in a very shallow way, or (3) paying attention to you. More energy and commitment is required to listen in an attending sort of way. You must move your mental focus from other things to what the speaker is saying. Rather than watching television and *hearing* the speaker, you will take your attention from the television and place it on the speaker.

Because attending requires you to move your focus away from what you were doing, there are times when you will be unable or unwilling to listen at the attending level. The excellent communicator often chooses to make this fact explicit by saying something like, "Gregory, I'd love to hear about the convention plans, and right now I'm trying to get these parts sorted. If you don't mind that I keep working, we can talk about this now. If you'd rather, I should be done with this job in 45 minutes and then I could give you my full attention." That allows the speaker to decide what level of listening attention his or her message requires.

IMPROVING ATTENDING

You can take certain steps to improve your listening at the attending level. The most important is to move your body so that you can comfortably make eye contact with the speaker. Remember that much of an interpersonal communication message comes from the nonverbal cues. Looking at the speaker will provide you with significantly more information.

Making eye contact will usually result in a second important way to improve your attending skills—facing the speaker makes it easier for your external ears to scoop up sound. You've probably noticed that dogs and cats move their ears around in order to focus on the sound waves they are receiving. Humans have only the most limited ability to move their ears separate from moving their heads. Even though that's true, the direction the ears are facing makes a tremendous difference in the amount you can hear. Here's a little exercise you can do to demonstrate this. While a friend is talking, take your hands and cup them around your ears to make a larger ear-like shell. The volume of your friend's voice will increase dramatically. Now put your cupped hands facing backward, as though you were a dog trying to hear something behind you. Your friend's voice will be very difficult to hear. Use this little experiment to remind yourself to get your ears around so they face the speaker.

A third way to improve listening at the attending level is to remove distractions. You might, for example, unplug your phone if calls keep interrupting your conversation. At home, turn off the television or turn the radio down. If other people are around, you might choose to move to a more private place. In a classroom, put your notes from other classes away so they don't distract you. All these ideas help you to keep your attention on the speaker.

Understanding

The next level of listening is understanding. *Understanding* requires the listener to make certain the **message is being decoded accurately**—in a way which matches the speaker's intent. In order to reach this level of listening, you must be willing to provide and ask for feedback. You must seek clarification.

Frequently in conversations, we listen only so we can respond. All the time the speaker is talking, we are putting together our rebuttal or thinking up the story we're going to share. We are not working to understand what the other person is saying. Rather we are thinking about our response to what we think the other person said. In order to reach the level of understanding, you must be willing to make sure you heard the message the way it was intended *before* you respond. Conversations held at the understanding level of listening tend to move more slowly. When the speaker is done speaking, the listener has to provide feedback about what he or she "thought" was said and verify that before moving to new material.

Listening to understand is appropriate in several situations: when instructions are being given, when cultural or language differences might lead to misunderstanding, or when emotions are running high. In each of these situations, the effective listener makes sure the decoding matches the intent of the encoding. The listener is careful not to jump to conclusions.

IMPROVING UNDERSTANDING

The surest way to reach this level of understanding is to provide feedback. Each time the speaker yields the floor, begin your response with either a very short summary of what you thought was said or with a question or statement of clarification.

Suppose your friend says, "I hear there are still tickets available for the play at the MoonLight Theater. I might try to get some for Saturday. What do you think?" In this very simple conversation, several potential miscommunications exist. Does "Saturday" mean afternoon or evening? Does "what do you think?" mean "do you think that would be a good idea" or does it mean "would you like to come?" How many tickets is "some?"

Here's another example. Suppose your boss asks you to "look into the possibility of marketing our products through direct mail." Does the boss mean *all* the company's products or only a certain group? Does "look into" mean "and prepare a written report?" By "direct mail" does the boss mean "a letter to customers on a mailing list" or "in a company-developed color catalog" or perhaps "as a product line in someone else's catalog?"

In those situations where listening to understand is important, you will need to admit that you are unsure what the intended message was. Such an admission makes people feel vulnerable. They must take a personal risk to admit a lack of understanding. In the U.S., knowing and knowledge are power. Not knowing and being unsure may be seen as weakness. Therefore, listening at the level of understanding is sometimes difficult. It asks something of you which you are not always willing to give. The excellent listener realizes the costs of misunderstanding are often much greater than the costs of appearing unknowledgeable. To understand, you must admit that you might not understand.

Remembering

The fourth level of listening difficulty is listening to remember. Are you paying enough attention and clarifying the message enough that you can **remember the relevant information in the future**?

Our brains work on two levels of remembering and processing information. The first level is short-term memory. The amount of information your brain can hold in short-term memory is limited. To use a computer analogy, there is a limit to the amount of RAM you have. In short-term memory, we keep the information we are currently using. For example, if you are a clerk in a store, you are actively using your knowledge of math when you count back change. You might also have the customer's name in short-term memory, and information about a special product she wants you to try and get for her. When your short-term memory is full, one of two things will happen—you can transfer the information to your long-term memory (somewhat like storing computer information on a disk) or you will begin forgetting things. Many people who have a great deal of information which they need in the short term, but do not want to transfer to long-term memory, make lists. A list allows you to forget without losing the information completely. You can put the information back in as you need it.

Listening to remember, that is, purposefully moving information to long-term memory, requires additional energy. It rarely happens without conscious effort.

IMPROVING REMEMBERING

You can use several methods which will help you move information to long-term memory so it won't get lost. The most natural method is to tie what you are hearing to information you already have stored. You might think of your long-term memory as being somewhat like a filing cabinet. If you already have a file in which you store this sort of information, it is easier and quicker to add a new piece of information than it would be to create a whole new file. So the fastest way to remember something is to think about how the new information is similar to and different from information you already know.

As you age and experience more, your filing cabinet grows larger. As a result, it is usually easier for older people to remember things than for younger people. You can observe this at school. Most of the time, the older students get the better grades. They may or may not work any harder at their lessons. The reality is, they have already created more files, so it's easier to find something to tie the new information to.

An exceedingly effective way to remember new information is to think up a **memory device**. For example, most English speakers remember the number of days in each month by remembering a little saying: thirty days hath September, April, June, and November. All the rest have 31, excepting February alone.

Many school children learn to spell "arithmetic" by remembering "A Rare Individual Thought He Might Eat Turkey In Church"—each word begins with the next letter in arithmetic. And the musical notes which correspond to the lines in written music are remembered by "Every Good Boy Does Fine" (or perhaps you were taught "every good boy deserves fudge"). You can consciously create memory devices for any kind of information you want to remember. A new school to teach international business people foreign languages is having great success with this approach. For example, the spelling of socks—SOCKS—is close in sound to the Spanish for "that's what it is." *Eso si, que es.* In order to learn to play a high enough card in the game of bridge, learners are told, "Never send a boy to do a man's job." The more colorful your memory devices, the more they will work well and rapidly for you.

Each of the levels of listening builds upon the one before it. In order to remember, you need first to hear and then to pay attention. If you want what you remember to be accurate, you need to understand the message clearly. There is one additional level of listening which, because it is so different from the usual types of listening we do, will be discussed in its own section.

ACTIVE LISTENING

Active listening is sometimes called empathic listening. This special kind of listening is appropriate when you are helping people solve problems which are very important to them. *Empathy* is described as listening **with the eyes/ears/feelings of the speaker**. It requires the listener to let go of his or her own experiences and to look at the world through the eyes of the speaker.

This final level of listening requires a significant additional commitment of time and energy. It is so difficult that few people become real experts at it. Management research indicates, however, that managers need to develop their active listening skills. Workers have problems, both personal and professional, which get in the way of their effective performance. Having someone listen actively can help them solve their problems and get back to work. In fact, active listening is such a powerful productivity tool that many organizations are teaching this listening skill to their managers.

In order to listen with empathy, you must accept certain assumptions about people and your relationships with them. These assumptions are:

Managers need to be counselors. Although some managers still believe workers are responsible for their problems and should leave them at home, modern managers have discovered that unsolved problems keep workers from being as effective as they could be. They believe it is the manager's job to take whatever action is necessary to help workers work effectively.

People know what is best for them. This assumption means that when a person has some problem, he or she also has the best answer to the problem. As an outsider, you cannot possibly have as good an understanding of a person's problem as he or she has. Given that, helping the other find his or her own solution is a much more practical use of time than trying to think up solutions yourself.

What is best for the other is ultimately best for you. Suppose an excellent employee has begun to do somewhat average work. You wonder what the problem is and so decide to talk to him about it. In the conversation, he says his parents have started making so many demands of him that he is becoming distracted. He says he has even considered moving to another town in order to put some distance between himself and his parents. He asks you what you think he should do.

Your internal response is a selfish one—you don't want to lose this excellent employee and have to find and train a replacement. Suppose you say you think he should stay—in fact, you will offer him a raise if he'll stay. Maybe he can use the extra money to take more vacations out of town, thus taking breaks from his parents. You think you have hit upon a very sensible, win-win solution. If, however, your employee follows your advice with reservations, finds the situation with his family worsens, and continues a downhill slide in productivity, you have not gained anything. Active listening takes the approach of helping the other find his own best solution.

The Goal of Active Listening

As an active listener, your goal is to help the speaker **clarify issues** and **clarify alternatives**. The job does not include thinking up solutions, no matter how many times the speaker says, "What do you think I should do?" If you are going to look at a situation through the eyes of someone else, it is irrelevant what you would do.

The Process of Active Listening

In active listening, you want to accomplish three goals:

- Encourage the speaker to talk enough that he or she can hear what the issues are,
- Clarify what the speaker is saying, and
- Reflect what you have heard the speaker say back to the speaker so that he or she can hear it.

Although it seems logically odd, people frequently don't know what they think about a really important issue. The more emotionally involved they are with an issue, the less likely they are to be able to sort out what they think without help. Active listening helps others figure out what they really think.

The Process of Actively Listening

Active listening is a process of three steps. They occur first in order and then they recur in different orders as the conversation continues.

WITHHOLDING JUDGMENT

The first step in active listening is to withhold all judgment or evaluation. Remember it is irrelevant what you think about the issue. Suppose an unmarried friend of yours is pregnant. She is very upset and doesn't know whether she should have an abortion, have the child and give it up for adoption, have the child and raise it herself, or marry the father and raise the child. Almost all of us have some opinion about this situation. Some have a very strong opinion. When we make the commitment to actively listen, we are choosing to give someone a very large gift. We are agreeing to listen without bringing ourselves into the picture. We are choosing to be absolutely selfless.

In some situations, this first step is too big. If you have such strong opinions on a particular topic that you cannot listen without judging, tell the speaker that, in this case, you are not a good person to talk with. Once you have made a commitment to listen without judgment, you must work very hard to keep your commitment.

HELPING THE SPEAKER SPEAK

The second step in the process of active listening is to help the speaker speak. For a variety of reasons, sometimes words just don't come out. One of those reasons is that we are used to taking turns in conversations—first we're the listener, then the speaker, then the listener, and so on. As the listener, you may need to give the speaker permission to continue speaking. Here are some ideas for helping the speaker speak.

- **Say "yes, and then . . .?"** That indicates that you have been listening and are willing to continue doing so.
- **Repeat the last three or four words the speaker said**, allowing your voice to trail off at the end. For example, suppose the speaker said, "and so that's how I've come to find myself in such an awful predicament with no apparent way out." You would say ". . . no apparent way out . . ." Either the speaker will begin again or you can just sit for a minute in silence. The quiet time will allow the speaker to think about possible ways. Soon, you'll find the speaker begins again, perhaps with something like, "Well, one solution I've been thinking about is . . ."

Common sense might lead you to ask a question of the talker like "What did you do then?" or "Who have you told about this?" Unless you believe you really need the answer to the question, avoid questions entirely. Here's why. They force a particular direction onto the conversation and may take the conversation away from the real issues. Here's an example. Suppose an employee has said to you he is having serious problems with his teenage son. Common sense would probably lead you to ask what kinds of problems he's having. Because it would be rude not to tell you since he brought the topic up, the conversation would go in the direction of the problems. Imagine an alternative situation. Rather than asking the question, suppose you say, "Yes, and . . .?" Your employee might say, "I wonder if I could start earlier on Tuesdays and leave by three so I can attend a counseling session. It would really help."

The second response you should avoid is any response which includes a value judgment. Even listeners who are doing an excellent job of keeping their own answers to themselves sometimes respond to the speaker in a way which indicates evaluation. For example, "Boy, that really is a predicament!" might on the surface seem like a supportive thing to say. To a sensitive speaker, it might sound like "Well, you made a bigger mess of things than I had imagined!" "Oh dear," and "you poor thing" are similar evaluative statements which do not necessarily convey the support you had intended to give.

CLARIFYING THE SPEAKER'S INTENT

The third step in active listening is to help the speaker clarify what is really going on inside. This clarifying step requires you to do two things.

The first is to listen to everything the speaker is telling you. That means you must listen beyond the words. You must listen to the voice quality, the body language, the silences. You must get the whole message.

The second part of clarifying the message is to tell the speaker what you think he or she has been saying. For example, you might say, "Jennifer, although you say you can get the project done by Tuesday, your voice and body don't reflect that. Is there something I should know?" Or as another example, you might say, "When I listen to you talk about these alternative solutions, I don't really hear any enthusiasm for any of them. Perhaps you haven't found the right solution yet. . ."

Active listening can be very tiring for both of the participants. For the speaker it is difficult to work on issues and for the listener it is difficult to remain uninvolved. When you are just learning active listening, keep your interactions short—maybe ten minutes or less. Even when you feel quite practiced in this advanced sort of listening, one hour is enough. If the speaker has not identified a good solution, make an appointment to talk again later. People who are tired are not at their problem-solving best.

In general, people's listening skills are poor. Very few of us feel that anyone ever really listens to us. The good news is that listening skills are learnable. And the more we can listen to each other, the more healthy and productive we will all be.

Several barriers get in the way of excellent listening. The difference between speaking rates and listening rates is one of them. Physical barriers, psychological barriers, and physiological barriers also make the listening a challenge.

Listening skills are additive. The skills learned for one kind of listening are helpful in increasingly complex levels of listening. The simplest kind of listening is hearing—actually receiving the physical sounds without too much distortion. Each of the next levels of listening requires a greater commitment of energy and caring. Attending requires the listener to devote energy to getting the message accurately, understanding asks the listener to hear the message as the sender intended it, and remembering requires that the listener link the new information to information already known so that it can be retrieved later. Each of these levels of listening requires incremental amounts of skills, energy, and practice.

The fifth and ultimate level of listening, active listening, requires a quantum leap in commitment to developing listening skills because it asks the listener to let go of all ego involvement. Every minute someone can listen at this level, the world becomes a better and healthier place. When you give the gift of listening without judgment, you help others heal themselves.

19

Oral Presentations

Written reports provide a record of an investigation that can be saved. It is information that is "documented." Obviously, documentation has great value. The problem with reports is that they are one-way communication. They tend to shut off discussion rather than encourage it.

As a result, many organizations prefer to have important information presented orally. The interactive channel allows receivers to question and provide feedback to the presenter. Formal presentations require special skills of the presenter. This chapter provides information to help you develop those skills.

PREPARING THE PRESENTATION

Most people find it very difficult to speak in front of others. In fact, in his article "Death Ranked Second," Gary Collier says that when Americans are asked to rank their fears, they put public speaking first. Public speaking is a skill, and like other skills, it can be improved rapidly by applying good techniques and practicing frequently.

A student was expressing his fears about public speaking. He said he had no trouble speaking to his classmates as long as he was sitting down. He wondered why speaking became so difficult when he had to stand up and face the very same classmates. The answer is actually easy: he has had many years of practice speaking from his desk and very little practice speaking while standing and looking at the entire classroom of students.

With practice and the suggestions made here, you will feel much more comfortable when called upon to make oral presentations to others.

Excellent oral presentations begin the way excellent written presentations do—with a consideration of the **presenter's goals** and the **audience's expectations**. In general, presentations have a persuasive element, so those principles that apply in writing persuasive messages will almost always play a role in oral presentation.

Analyze the Audience

If you don't know who will be attending your presentation, ask. Imagine how uncomfortable you would feel if you thought the audience was going to be fellow students, and the university president and members of the local press showed up hoping to see how students are performing in the classroom! The same thing can happen at work. Think about your audience before you begin.

Because there will be many people in your audience, your audience-analysis task will be made easier if you focus on the decision makers in the group. Ask yourself "Who is going to take action on this proposal or information?" Then consider everything you know about that person or persons. What is his or her thinking style? How much does he or she know about the topic already? How busy is the audience? What is the audience used to or expecting? How much credibility do you have with this audience?

It also helps to consider every presentation as the answer to a question. Some questions might be: How can we improve listening skills? Why are some communicators better than others? How can a writer change the tone of a message? The more specifically you state the question, the more likely you will be to address the decision makers' concerns.

Base Your Argument on What Is Important to the Audience

If you are hoping to persuade your audience to some action, you will need to present your argument in terms important to the audience. Suppose that relieving stress is very important to the audience. That becomes a criterion by which the audience evaluates your ideas. You can use criteria to set the structure of your presentation. Remember to use language that includes the listeners (you-attitude) and makes them and their needs and interests central—just as you do in writing.

Say Enough but Not Too Much

Oral presentations work best when they center around **one main point**. First state the main point, then offer **parallel support** for your point. Parallel support means that each of your support ideas should be phrased in a grammatically parallel way. In addition, if you give two examples of how your first idea supports your main theme, then give two examples for each of your other ideas. For example, if your main point is that "a writer can easily change the tone of a message," supporting points might be "by writing shorter sentences," "by substituting positive words for negative or neutral ones," and "by using more you-attitude". Parallel support is easier for listeners to follow.

Using the **rule of three** also makes presentations easier to follow. The Rule of Three is a very old storytelling structure where three ideas or alternatives are offered and discussed. The *Three Little Pigs* is one example of a story using this structure. The wolf visits each of three pigs sequentially. In fairy tales, the fairy always allows three wishes. In jokes, the punch line always comes at the end of the third variation of the story. In fact, the rule of three is such a part of our mythical history that we believe the number 3 has special power.

Whether or not you believe there is magic in threes, the success of the rule of three in storytelling at least suggests that people can comfortably remember three things. Therefore, structuring your report so that your main idea is supported by three subpoints is especially helpful.

Check Your Logic

As you structure your presentation, make sure you are being logical. A clear, logical flow of ideas will help your audience follow you. Since the audience can't rewind and replay your presentation if they get confused, don't let faulty logic make understanding you difficult.

For example, cause-effect links are good, but avoid confusing symptoms with causes. Here's an example of someone confusing symptom and cause: On a hot day, the car overheated. The mechanic noticed immediately that the fan belt was broken. He replaced the fan belt, assuming that would fix the cause of the overheating. Two days later, the fan belt broke again. Upon further inspection, the mechanic discovered that the broken fan belt was a symptom of a pulley system that was not perfectly aligned. The pulleys were the cause. Both the broken fan belts and the overheating were symptoms.

Chronological organization is good, but when you use it, make certain that everything is chronological. You will confuse those listening to you if most of your presentation is chronological but not all of it. When you use a time-based, sequential organizational style, stick with it.

Don't confuse correlation with causality. One event happening after another does not guarantee that the two are causally related. For example, a study of newborns in northern California observed that babies born to mothers who did not have health insurance suffered significantly higher infant mortality rates than babies born to mothers who were insured. The study demonstrated faulty logic when it concluded that "lack of health insurance is resulting in serious illness and death." It is more likely that mothers without health insurance had very little prenatal health care. Poor prenatal care may indeed result in babies at higher risk.

Create a Compelling Beginning

The beginning of an oral presentation is so important that it requires special attention. All the people at a presentation left other activities to attend it. They are likely to be thinking initially about things other than your topic. You need to start in a way that draws the focus to yourself and your topic. A good beginning is one that interests the audience and sets the tone for the rest of the presentation. To do this, the beginning must include **what** the presentation is about and **why** it is important; it must **establish rapport** with the audience; it must show **how** you will develop your argument; and when necessary, it must provide evidence of your **credibility** to speak on this topic. That's a tall order.

If someone else has not introduced you, you must introduce yourself. Begin with "Hello, I'm _____." Then perhaps you can add a brief statement about why you are qualified to speak on this topic: "As part of my major in pre-law, I have reviewed the new credit application law." Follow with a statement of why the presentation is important to the audience: "I want to discuss with you how it might change the way you write credit refusal letters." Listeners appreciate having your recommendation or conclusion up front. They then know where the presentation is going and can more easily follow your logic.

Make your beginning interesting. You want to help the audience relax so that you and they can enjoy the process. The beginning needs to be long enough that the audience can get settled without missing any of the real content of your presentation.

Use Transitions Generously

Repetition, review, and transitions increase the likelihood that your audience will understand and remember what you say. When you are gaining information from a written document, you can reread to improve your comprehension. However, when the information is presented orally, the listener can't "go back" to missed information, so the presenter needs to build in some amount of repetition and review to keep the audience following along.

A standard piece of public-speaking advice is to (1) tell the audience what you are going to tell them, (2) tell them, and (3) tell them what you told them. As long as you apply this advice with some grace and subtlety, it works well.

Transition words like *however, therefore, as you can see,* and *in conclusion* verbally indicate the structure of your presentation. They show the audience the relationships you want them to see. The more of these transition words and phrases you can build into your presentation, the better. You can also show the organization of your presentation by saying things like "First I want to show you the results from last quarter." "This second piece of information came from the Census Department." "Third, and finally, you can see in this pie chart published in the *Wall Street Journal*." Each of these devices makes your structure obvious to your listeners and reduces the work they must do to follow you.

Prepare Appropriate Visuals

Because people remember best what they see *and* hear, almost all business presentations include visual aids. The goal is to create visuals which add value to your presentation and increase your persuasiveness.

If you are giving a presentation to an audience that will perceive that you have an accent, visual aids can serve an additional function. They can train your audience to understand your accent. At the beginning of your presentation, use a visual aid that presents several ideas you plan to address. As you introduce your topic, the audience can compare your pronunciation with the written words. After only a minute or two, the audience will be able to follow you easily.

Essentially, visual aids can be grouped into three types, each of which has a different purpose and different design requirements.

TEXT VISUALS

Text visuals contain only words and are most effective as a "map" of your presentation. Use action phrases, not full sentences, and limit the number of lines of text on any one visual. Three ideas per visual is enough. **Do not read your visual text to the audience.** Instead, talk about the topics on the visual. Keep the phrases on your visual parallel and put them in the order you will address them. Using upper- and lowercase letters, bold print, or color can add emphasis to your points.

Make certain the writing on your visual aid is large enough for all members of the audience to read. Standard typewriter text is not large enough. You can easily make your typesize larger by making an enlarged copy on a copy machine. You will need to make your margins larger before you enlarge your type. If you don't, the letters will be enlarged right off the paper, slide, or overhead.

CONCEPTUAL VISUALS

Conceptual visuals use pictures or designs, typically to show the relationships of ideas. Because many people process information visually, a picture is often more memorable. Conceptual visuals are especially helpful in training. Use a concept you believe the audience already understands to teach them about a new concept. For example, a picture of an ancient bonsai tree might be an effective visual to show while introducing the goal of organizational renewal versus a more traditional goal of organizational growth. If you want to address the topic of international trade in a boundaryless world, you might show a picture of Earth taken from outer space. If you want to talk about the health costs that result from stress, you might prepare a visual aid using a "Get Well Soon" card—perhaps a funny drawing of an elephant in bed with a thermometer in its mouth.

People respond well to images. They enjoy seeing relationships demonstrated visually. Many business presenters use too few conceptual visuals. Try to include more of them in your presentations. Your audience will appreciate it.

CHARTS OR GRAPHS

Charts or graphs show relationships and are especially valuable for transmitting complex numerical information. Line charts, bar charts, and pie charts are the most frequently used formats. Although tables allow you to give your audience exact numbers for a large number of variables, most people do not easily see relationships when they are confronted with columns of numbers. You will be more effective if you communicate numerical data using charts or graphs. As a guideline, convey only one message per chart. Bar charts are best for showing comparisons of several items. Column charts and time lines show change in one or several variables over time. Pie charts show the relation of one part to others as well as to the whole. A complete pie represents 100 percent of something, and each "slice" represents the percentage a particular part contributes to the whole.

Label your visual aids meaningfully. Horizontally typed headings and labels are preferable to vertical labels. Limit the number of colors, patterns, or type styles on any one visual.

Avoid using red and green on the same visual aid. As was discussed in Chapter 16, a very large number of people, especially males, have red-green color blindness. Since they find it difficult to tell the two colors apart, they may miss your point if one of your time-series lines is red and the other green. Instead, use blue, purple, or black with either red or green. Avoid yellow. It doesn't show up well in large rooms with the lights on.

Keep your text large enough to read easily. And check your spelling and numbers very carefully.

PREPARE NOTE CARDS

Once you have organized your presentation, you are ready to prepare note cards. The first goal is to make your note cards look professional. Use note cards rather than paper. Paper is more apt to make noise as you move it around. The sheets of thin paper are more likely to stick together than note cards. Note cards hold their shape nicely in your hand if you don't have a lectern to place them on.

You can use any of the standard-size note cards. White is preferable. It is also better to use cards with the back side line-free.

Write your notes on the front side only. The side facing the audience should be clean and clear. Note cards are called that because they contain only notes, not full speech text. When you have the entire speech written out before you, it is nearly impossible not to read it. The problem with reading your presentation is that people never read with the same voice intonation and energy that they speak with. The audience becomes bored much sooner when you read.

Instead, use your note cards for notes that will remind you of what you are going to say and the order you are going to say it in. Double- or triple-space. Use writing or type large enough to read from cards held slightly above your waist.

Number your cards clearly in the upper right corner. Note cards have been dropped by presenters before you. It's helpful to be able to put them immediately back in order. On your note cards, you can make a notation at each point in the presentation when you plan to use a visual aid.

REHEARSE

Once you have prepared your presentation and made your note cards, you are ready to begin practicing presenting. Many presenters spend nearly as much time practicing their presentations as they do preparing them. And the time is well spent.

Rehearsing allows you to feel comfortable, with your material and with the concept of presenting to an audience. Your purpose is not to memorize the presentation but rather to become comfortable and deliver your message smoothly. Even if you are not particularly anxious, rehearse at least three times—once alone facing a mirror, then before a supportive listener, and finally in front of two or three friends.

Each time you rehearse, rehearse out loud. Reading your presentation over in your head does no good. If you do not practice out loud, your voice will scare you, and you will trip over words. There will be rough spots. Rehearsing standing up, facing whatever audience you can find, and talking out loud will make a big difference in your confidence level on presentation day.

If your presentation includes visual aids, be sure to include them in your practice. In your final rehearsal, try to use the room where you will actually be making your presentation.

Time your presentation. If you have been given a specific speaking time, make certain you do not run over. Edit if you need to. The audience will become very anxious if you are going over the time they expected you to speak. When the audience is anxious, you are very likely to sense that anxiousness. You will become increasingly nervous.

Give some thought to your nonverbals while you are practicing. Stand up straight with your weight balanced evenly on both feet. Some people are unconscious toe-tappers. It is difficult to tap your toes if your weight is firmly on both feet. Some people are rockers. When they get nervous, they rock back and forth. Ask your friends to give you feedback about your body movements.

Good posture gives the impression of confidence and authority. It also allows you to breathe deeply and easily, which keeps your voice strong and your tension down. Smile. Make eye contact with your audience (but avoid staring at just one or two members of the audience). Dress neatly, cleanly, and conservatively. Jewelry should be small; especially avoid jewelry that makes noise. You don't want bracelets that jangle, for example. If your hair is long, use clips or hair spray to keep it back from your face. Avoid touching your hair or face. Frequently, men with mustaches and beards stroke their facial hair without knowing it. Thinking about these things while you practice will result in better nonverbals during your presentation.

Sometimes the arrangement of the room is fixed. In such cases, make sure you are not standing between the audience and your visuals, and move so you can make eye contact with your audience. If the arrangement of the room is not fixed, take charge of it. Move chairs, tables, visual aids to create the atmosphere you prefer.

ON THE BIG DAY

You can do several things to improve the quality of your presentation in the few minutes right before you "go on." First, check to make certain any equipment you need is there and working properly. Do this early enough to get replacement equipment or find an alternative room if something is wrong.

Do not chew gum. Sometimes chewing gum helps reduce the tension that frequently builds right before a presentation. However, you must remember to throw it out before you approach the front of the room.

Do not drink any cold liquid. You want your throat to be relaxed so your voice will sound strong. Cold liquids tend to tighten the throat. Also be careful of drinking coffee or tea with caffeine. Caffeine may contribute to nervousness. In addition, it causes your mouth to be dry, which will interfere with your voice quality and feeling of comfort. The very best prepresentation drink is warm water with lemon and honey.

Remember to breathe. If your lungs are full of air, your voice will be strong. A strong, confident voice will help your audience to relax. As soon as the audience is relaxed, you will relax. And remember to smile as you say "Hello, my name is . . ."

*A*lthough many people avoid public speaking, you are very likely to be called upon to give professional presentations. Both the quality of your presentations and the confidence with which you face them will improve as you practice this communication skill.

To prepare effective presentations, begin with an analysis of the decision makers in your audience. Use language and logic to make the structure of your presentation clear. Try to keep your ideas limited to three. Use visual aids to support your message.

To present effective presentations, rehearse out loud and often. Avoid cold drinks. Keep your posture confident and competent. If you appear relaxed, your audience will relax.

Bibliography

**General
Communication**

Adler, Ronald B., & Neil Towne. *Looking Out, Looking In*, 7th Ed., Harcourt Brace Jovanovich: Fort Worth, TX, 1993.

Alberti, Robert E., & Michael L. Emmons. *Your Perfect Right: a guide to assertive living*, 5th Ed., Impact Publishers: San Luis Obispo, CA, 1986.

Arapakis, Maria. *Softpower! How to speak up, set limits, and say no without losing your lover, your job, or your friends*, Warner Books: New York, 1990.

Baldrige, Letitia. *Letitia Baldrige's Complete Guide to Executive Manners*, Rawson Associates: New York, 1985.

Chapman, Elwood N. *Your Attitude Is Showing: a primer of human relations*, 6th Ed., Macmillan: New York, 1991.

Covey, Stephen R. *The 7 Habits of Highly Effective People: powerful lessons in personal change*, Simon & Schuster: New York, 1990.

DeVito, Joseph A. *Essentials of Human Communication*, HarperCollins: New York, 1993.

Fisher, Roger, & Scott Brown. *Getting Together: building a relationship that gets to yes*, Houghton Mifflin: Boston, 1988.

Fisher, Roger, & William Ury. *Getting to Yes: negotiating agreement without giving in*, Houghton Mifflin: Boston, 1981.

Gouran, Dennis S., Larry D. Miller, & William E. Weithoff. *Mastering Communication,* Allyn and Bacon: Boston, 1992.

Harvard Business Review, eds. *The Articulate Executive: improving written, interpersonal, and group communication*, Harvard Business School: Boston, 1991.

Hirschhorn, Larry. *Managing in the New Team Environment: skills, tools, and methods*, Addison-Wesley: Reading, Mass., 1991.

John-Roger & Peter McWilliams. *Wealth 101: Getting what you want, enjoying what you've got*, Prelude Press: Los Angeles, 1992.

Johnson, David W. *Reaching Out: interpersonal effectiveness and self-actualization*, 4th Ed., Prentice Hall: Englewood Cliffs, NJ, 1990.

Kao, John J. *Managing Creativity*, Prentice Hall: Englewood Cliffs, N.J., 1991.

Lewis, Chad T., Joseph E. Garcia, & Sarah M. Jobs. *Managerial Skills in Organizations*, Allyn and Bacon: Boston, 1990.

Lustig, Myron W. & Jolene Koester. *Intercultural Competence: interpersonal communication across cultures*, HarperCollins: New York, 1993.

McManus, Jason, Editor. *Time Retrospective: communication 1940-1989*, Time Inc. Magazines: Rockaway, NJ, 1989.

Smith, Alvie L. *Innovative Employee Communication: new approaches to improving trust, teamwork, and performance*, Prentice Hall: Englewood Cliffs, NJ, 1991.

U.S. Department of Labor. *Opportunity 2000: creating affirmative action strategies for a changing workforce*, U.S. Government Printing Office: Washington, D.C., 1988.

VanOosting, James. *Practicing Business: communication in the workplace*, Houghton Mifflin: Boston, 1992.

Vesper, Joan, & Vincent Ryan Ruggiero. *Contemporary Business Communication: from thought to expression*, HarperCollins: New York, 1993.

Grammar and Style

Brusaw, Charles T., Gerald J. Alred, & Walter E. Olin. *The Business Writer's Handbook*, 2nd Ed., St. Martin's Press: New York, 1982.

Ellsworth, Blanche. *English Simplified*, 6th Ed., Harper & Row: New York, 1990.

Garner, Bryan A. *A Dictionary of Modern Legal Usage*, Oxford University Press: Oxford, 1990.

Lanham, Richard A. *Revising Business Prose*, 2nd Ed., Macmillan Publishing: New York, 1987.

Miller, Casey, & Kate Swift. *The Handbook of Nonsexist Writing: for writers, editors and speakers*, 2nd Ed., Harper & Row: New York, 1988.

Oxford University Press Editors. *A Concise Dictionary of Business*, Oxford University Press: Oxford, 1991.

Thomas, Susan G. *Grammar and Punctuation Essentials for Business Communication*, South-Western: Cincinnati, 1992.

Written Communication

Andrew, Deborah C., & William D. Andrews. *Business Communication*, 2nd Ed., Macmillan Publishing: New York, 1993.

Bailey, Edward P. *The Plain English Approach to Business Writing*, Oxford University Press, 1990.

Estrin, Herman A., & Norbert Elliot. *Technical Writing in the Corporate World: basic strategies for success*, Crisp Publications: Los Altos, CA, 1990.

Flesch, Rudolf. *Say What You Mean*, Harper & Row: New York, 1972.

Friedlander, Edward Jay, & John Lee. *Feature Writing for Newspapers and Magazines: the pursuit of excellence*, HarperCollins: New York, 1993.

Goldfinger, Edward. *A Better Way of Writing*. South-Western: Cincinnati, 1987.

Weiss, Edmond H. *Writing Remedies: practical exercises for technical writing*, Oryx: Phoenix, AZ, 1990.

Wilcox, Dennis L., Phillip H. Ault, & Warren K. Agee. *Public Relations: strategies and tactics*, 3rd Ed., HarperCollins: New York, 1992.

Employment

Bixler, Susan. *The Professional Image*, The Putnam Publishing Group: New York, 1984.

Bolles, Richard Nelson. *What Color is Your Parachute: a practical manual for job-hunters and career-changers*, Ten Speed Press: Berkeley, 1993.

Curtis, Dan B., James J. Floyd, & Jerry L. Winsor. *Interpersonal Communication and the Business Interview*, HarperCollins: New York, 1993.

Einhorn, Lois J., Patricia Hayes Bradley, & John E. Baird, Jr. *Effective Employment Interviewing: unlocking human potential,* Scott, Foresman and Company: Glenview, IL, 1982.

Elsea, Janet G. *First Impression, Best Impression: learn the secret of making a lasting impression in the four minutes that can make or break you,* Simon & Schuster: New York, 1984.

Irish, Richard K. *Go Hire Yourself an Employer*, 3rd Ed., Doubleday: New York, 1987.

King, Norman. *The First Five Minutes: the successful opening moves in business, sales and interviews*, Prentice Hall Press: New York, 1987.

Wilkes, Mary, & C. Bruce Crosswait. *Professional Development: the dynamics of success,* 4th Ed., Harcourt Brace Jovanovich: San Diego, 1991.

Verbal Communication

Elgin, Suzette Haden. *Success with the Gentle Art of Verbal Self Defense*, Prentice Hall: Englewood Cliffs, NJ, 1989.

Ryckman, W. G. *The Art of Speaking Effectively*, Dow Jones-Irwin: Homewood, IL, 1983.

Tannen, Deborah. *You Just Don't Understand: women and men in conversation*, Ballantine Books: New York, 1990.

Tannen, Deborah. *That's Not What I Meant: how conversational style makes or breaks relationships*, Ballantine Books: New York, 1986.

Vasile, Albert J., & Harold K. Mintz. *Speak with Confidence: a practical guide*, HarperCollins: New York, 1993.

Technology and Communication

Gerstein, Marc S. *The Technology Connection: strategy and change in the information age*, Addison Wesley: Reading, MA, 1987.

Manges, Michele. "Junk mail in the age of FAX," *Wall Street Journal*, May 3, 1989, p. B1.

Index

Business letters. (*cont.*)
    modified-block letter format, 53
    of inquiry about employment opportuni-
       ties, 105–6
    nonverbals of, 46–48
    ordering, confirming, and acknowledg-
       ing letters, 64–65
    parts of, 48, 51
    requesting information, 65–66
       response to, 69
    routine claims and adjustments, 66–67
Business Periodicals Index, 114

Call for action, in persuasive messages,
    88–90
Call for Bids (CFBs), 155
Career counselors, 104
cc, 50
Channels of communication, 3–4
Charts, 193
Checkpoints, in instructions, 99
Claims, routine, and adjustments, 66–67
Clarity, 35–37
    in cross-cultural communication, 10–11
Closed punctuation, 50
Color, as attention-getting device, 86
Communication
    channels of, 3–4
    definition of, 2–3
    effective, 2
Company policy, avoiding reliance on,
    when saying no, 75
Comparison in instructions, 96
Completeness, 37–38
Complimentary close, 49
Conciseness, 38–39
Concreteness, 7, 37
    in cross-cultural communication, 10
Confidence, 40–41
Confirmation, letters of, 64–65
Congratulations letters, 63–64
Connotative meaning, 6–7
Content, adapting to the audience and, 21
Contractions
    conversational tone and, 41–42
    tone of written communication and, 20
Conversational tone, 41–42
Correctness, 39
Courtesy titles, 49
Cover letters. *See* Job application letters

Dangling prepositions, conversational tone
    and, 41–42
Dateline, 48
Decision tree, 35–36
Denotative meaning, 6–7
Diagrams, in instructions, 97
Direct message strategy, 58–71
    additional information in, 60–62
    forward-looking goodwill close in,
      62–64
    general advice on, 59
    immediate beginning in, 59–60
    ordering, confirming, and acknowledg-
      ing letters, 64–65
    positive responses to request, 67–68
    routine claims and adjustments, 66–67
    situations for, 59
Drawings, in instructions, 97
Dressing for job interviews, 144–45
Dynamic nature of communication, 3

Effective communication, 2
Emotions, connotative meaning and, 6–7
Empathy index, 25
Emphasis, position of, 31–33
Employers, looking for potential, 110
Employment communication. *See also* Job
    application letters; Résumé
    beginning the job search, 110–11
    making plan and, 107–10
    research and, 105–7
    setting goals and, 103–7
Enclosures, 50
End dating, in persuasive messages, 89
End of a communication, 32
Envelopes, 57
Ethical considerations, 12–13
Examples
    in cross-cultural communication, 10–11
    in instructions, 97
Executive stationery, 47
Executive summary, 165–66
Expert opinion, in attention-getting begin-
    nings, 85–86

Face-to-face communication, 4–5
Facts
    in attention-getting beginnings, 84–85
    in résumé, 121